ESSENTIAL BLACKJACK WISDOM

ABOUT THE AUTHOR

Avery Cardoza is the foremost authority on gambling in the world and best-selling author of 21 gaming books and advanced strategies. His company, Cardoza Publishing, founded in 1981, represents the top authors and experts in their fields. More than 200 titles and 9,000,000 books sold make Cardoza Publishing the world's largest and most respected seller of gaming books.

Cardoza's life has been unique among all gambling writers or players in that he has counted on his gambling winnings and activities as his only source of income throughout his adult life and before. In fact, has never had a 9-5 job. Though originally from New York City, where he is occasionally found, Cardoza has used his winnings to pursue a lifestyle of extensive traveling which has included extended sojourns in such exotic locales as Bahia in Brazil, Jerusalem, Tokyo, Greece, Southeast Asia as well as California, New Orleans, and of course, Las Vegas, where he did extensive research into the mathematical, emotional, and psychological aspects of winning.

Check out Avery Cardoza's new online gaming magazines at www.cardozaonline.com.

ESSENTIAL BLACKJACK WISDOM

Avery Cardoza

CARDOZA PUBLISHING

Cardoza Publishing is the foremost gaming and gambling publisher in the world with a library of more than 200 up-to-date and easy-to-read books and strategies. These authoritative works are written by the top experts in their fields and with more than 9,000,000 books in print, represent the best-selling and most popular gaming books anywhere.

to jes

FIRST EDITION
3rd Printing

Library of Congress Catalog Card No: 2002101906
ISBN:1-58042-060-5

Visit our website at www.cardozapub.com or write
for a full list of books and advanced,strategies.

CARDOZA PUBLISHING

PO Box 1500, Cooper Station, New York, NY 10276
Toll Free Phone (800)577-WINS
email: cardozapub@aol.com
www.cardozapub.com

TABLE OF CONTENTS

1

THE INTRODUCTION

This book is jam-packed with the knowledge and wisdom you need to win money at blackjack!

You'll learn the basics of play, rules, and general winning strategies to be able to beat casino blackjack, plus I'll provide you with a Master Chart of all the correct plays for single and multiple deck blackjack. You'll also learn from three chapters featuring a wealth of tips on game situations–7 on money management, 17 on basic plays, and 15 on general situations essential to winning.

And then, to further reinforce and test your knowledge, I have set up 70 challenging and instructive play-by-play hands in a fun question and answer format that covers *every* real situation exactly as you'll face in casino blackjack. I give you a hand–what are you going to do: hit, stand, double, split?

How good are you as a blackjack player right now?

We'll find out! You keep track of the answers to our 70 play-by-play situations, and then check your score in the back. That will let you know exactly where you're at right now. Are you ready to play for real money?

Are you pro level? Or do you need more study before risking money at the game? One pass through this book will give you the answers to these questions.

How good will you get? That's up to you. I have made it easy for you to take your game to the next level. If you're looking to be a winner at blackjack, let's move on my friend, and let me guide you to that promised land.

THE PLAY-BY-PLAY APPROACH

What I've done in this book, is show you the reasoning *behind* the moves you make at blackjack. Every strategy play is explained in clear language so you learn how to think like a winner. I not only give you the correct answer directly underneath each situation but tell you why it is the correct play and what thinking and concepts were involved in that strategy.

I've posed each situation in question form, sometimes leading you along a certain path of thinking. Aha—but keep your mind focused on the question itself, for you must rely on the sound thinking behind a blackjack strategy and not how the question may be posed.

This book is designed for multiple passes through it, with each pass designed to make you a better player.

FIRST TIME THROUGH THE BOOK

Don't worry if you don't know all the correct plays the first time through the book, for in each situation, as I've stated above, I'll show you the right play, *why* it should be made, and how to think when you're presented with the situation. You'll learn to develop "blackjack common sense"–the way to think and play like a winner. Your skill level will go up as will your profits.

SECOND TIME THROUGH THE BOOK

The first time should be fun, seeing how good you are at blackjack. The second time through, however, is the time to get serious and see how much you have improved, and even more importantly, how close you are to being ready to play for real money.

I have set up a scoring system to give you a sense of how prepared you *really* are to hit the tables. There is a grade given for the number of questions answered correctly. Forget how good you think you are. Your grade will be your grade. If it is not as high as you think it should be, then obviously, you need more work to make it better.

THE GOAL

The goal in these quizzes is to score 100%, to get everything right. You may ask, "Why is 95% not good enough?" In school, that would be an excellent score for anyone but a perfectionist, but in blackjack, anything less than perfect gives an edge back to the casino.

With just a little work, you should be able to achieve that perfect score. And that's our goal–to make you a perfect Basic Strategy player and a winner.

Many of the questions are easy, or at least I should say, they should be common sense to the learned blackjack player. But there are tough situations you will face as well. Your goal, again, is to get every question right so that you can win money at the tables.

NOTE ABOUT THE BOOK

I put all the information on one page to make it convenient for you, but you may cover the bottom with a sheet of paper while you answer the question, then uncover it, to see how you did.

The correct answers to all the plays in this book assume normal blackjack rules and knowledge of only three cards, the dealer's upcard and the player's two cards.*

Since 10s, Jacks, Queens and Kings are all valued equally as 10 points, I will use the term "10" or "10 value card" interchangeably to indicate any of those cards. For example, if I say the dealer has a 10, I may mean a King as easily as a 10, since they are both of the same value.

There is some repetition in this book, as particular concepts overlap on essential issues that are too important to address just once, but I have done this consciously, to help make you a better player.

With that said, let's get started on the road to winning.

*Games that allow doubling after splitting, surrender, and other options not normally encountered may call for different plays, depending upon the situation. Also, note that card counters will sometimes make plays contrary to the basic strategy plays, drawing on knowledge unavailable to the average player to improve on the basic strategy plays for a higher winning percentage.

2

THE BASICS OF BLACKJACK

BASICS & OBJECT OF THE GAME

You get two cards to start, as does the dealer. Your goal is to beat the dealer by either getting a higher total than the dealer without exceeding 21 or by the dealer exceeding 21 points first. If you have a higher point total, you win; if the dealer has a higher total, he wins. If you both have the same total, the hand is a tie, called a **push** at blackjack, nobody wins.

Going over 21 is called **busting** and is an automatic loser. If you bust, you lose, even if the dealer busts as well afterwards. That's your only disadvantage as a player. If the dealer busts, and you're still in the game, you win.

THE CARDS

Casinos use one, two, four, six and sometimes as many as eight decks of cards in their blackjack games. Blackjack played with a single deck of cards is called a **single deck** game, and with two or more decks, is called a **multiple deck** game.

Each deck is a standard pack of 52 cards, consisting of four cards of each value, Ace through King. Suits have no relevance in blackjack. Only the numerical value of the cards count.

When one or two decks are used, the dealer holds the cards in his hand. When more than two decks are used, the cards are dealt from a rectangular plastic or wooden device known as a **shoe**.

Each card in the deck is counted at face value; a 2 equals two points, a 3 equals three points, and a 9 equals nine points. The face cards, Jack, Queen and King, are counted as 10 points.

The Ace can be counted as 1 point or 11 points, at your discretion. When the Ace is counted as 11 points, that hand is called **soft**, as in the hand Ace, 7, *soft 18*. All other totals, including hands where the Ace counts as 1 point, are called hard, as in the hand 10, 6, A, *hard 17*.

BLACKJACK–AUTOMATIC WINNER

If your original two card hand contains an Ace with any 10 or face card (J, Q, K), the hand is called a **blackjack** and is an automatic winner for you paying 3-2 on your bet! (Some casinos pay only 6-5.) However, if the dealer gets a blackjack, he wins only what you have bet.

PAYOFFS

All other winning bets are paid off at even money. For every $1 bet, you win an equal amount. Thus, if you have a $5 bet on the table and win, you receive the original $5 back and $5 in winnings for a total of $10.

PLAYER OPTIONS

You go first in blackjack. You get dealt two cards, as does the dealer and can choose from the following options in playing your hand:

1. Hitting (Drawing) - You take one or more additional cards until you are satisfied with your total. (However, should you go over 21, you are busted and automatically lose.)

2. Standing - You take no more cards and stay with the total you have.

3. Doubling - You double your bet and must take one more card.

4. Splitting - If you have two cards of equal value (such as two sixes), you can split them into two separate hands, putting an equal amount of money on each hand. Cards may be resplit. Thus, if you receive an eight to your split eights, you can make a third split hand of eights. Note that Aces may be split only once and that if you receive a ten on a split ace it is only a 21, not a blackjack.

5. Surrender - (Rarely offered). You can forfeit your hand along with half your bet.

FACE UP CARDS OR FACE DOWN

In games using four or more decks, your cards are typically dealt face up. In single and double deck games, your cards will be dealt face down. Whether your cards are dealt face up or face down is unimportant because the dealer is bound by strict rules from which he cannot deviate.

SIGNALING YOUR OPTIONS
When the Cards Are Dealt Face Down
When the cards are dealt face down, you hold the cards in your hand to see what was dealt.

To *draw* a card, scrape the felt surface of the table with your cards and the dealer will respond by giving you a card. You may draw as many times as you like – until you bust.

To *stand*, slide the cards under your bet.

To *double down*, turn your cards over placing them face up in front of your bet. Put an additional bet equal to the original bet so that there are two equal stacks side by side. The dealer will deal one card face down, usually slipping that card under your bet. You may look at that card if you so desire.

To *split*, turn your pair face up, separating them buy a few inches so that the two cards form two separate hands. Then place a bet equal to the original bet behind the second card. Each hand is now played separately, using finger and hand signals to indicate hitting and standing decisions.

When the Cards Are Dealt Face Up
When the cards are dealt face up, you are not supposed to touch them and instead will signal all options using hand and finger signals.

To *draw* a card, scratch the felt with your fingers or point toward the card and the dealer will respond by giving you another card. You may keep drawing until satisfied.

To *stand*, wave your hand palm down over the cards and the dealer will move on the next player, or if there are none, to his own hand.

To *double down* or *split*, place an additional bet next to your original one. This indicates to the dealer that you are choosing one of those options. When you have a hand that could be both split or doubled, such as 55, the dealer will ask which option you prefer.

Insurance

When the dealer shows an Ace as the exposed card, you are offered an option called **Insurance**. This is a bet that the dealer has a 10-value card underneath his Ace for a blackjack. You can bet up to one half your original bet and will get paid 2 to 1 if you are correct. Note: Unless you are a card counter, insurance is a terrible bet and shouldn't be made.

The insurance wager is made by placing a bet of up to one-half your wager in the area marked "insurance." This is located on the layout above your bet.

THE DEALER'S RULES

Once all players have completed their turns, it is the dealer's turn. The dealer must draw to any hands 16 or below and stand on any total 17-21. The dealer has no options and cannot deviate from these rules.

In some casinos the dealer must draw to a **soft** 17–a total reached when the Ace is valued at 11 points such as the hand A 6.

THE PLAY OF THE GAME

The dealer will shuffle the cards after each round of cards and begin dealing from his left (your right) in a clockwise direction, dealing one card to each player and then himself, and then a second card. The dealer's second card will be face up and all players can use that knowledge to their advantage when choosing the best option to play in their own hand.

You must make your bets before the cards are dealt. If you forget to do so, the dealer will remind you that a bet is due.

If the dealer's upcard is an Ace, he will ask if players want insurance. If the dealer has a blackjack, all players that did not take insurance lose their bets. Players that took insurance break even on the play. If the dealer doesn't have a blackjack, he collects the lost insurance bets and play continues.

The procedures vary when the dealer shows a 10-value card. In many Nevada casinos the dealer must check his hole card for an Ace. If he has a blackjack, all player bets are lost unless a player himself has a blackjack. (Players can't insure against a 10-value card.)

If the dealer doesn't have a blackjack, he will face the first player and await that player's decision. Play begins with the bettor on the dealer's left, in the position known as **first base** and moves to each player in turn in a clockwise direction, until all players have acted upon their hands.

Now it is the dealer's turn. He will turn his hole card over so that all players can view both of his cards. He must play his hand according to the strict guidelines regulating his play; drawing to 17, then standing. If the dealer busts, all players still in the game for that round of play win automatically.

After playing his hand, the dealer will turn over each player's cards in turn, going counterclockwise from his right to his left, the opposite direction from how he dealt, paying the winners, and collecting from the losers.

When the round has been completed, all players must place a new bet before the next deal.

ENTERING A GAME

Find yourself any unoccupied seat at a blackjack table and make yourself comfortable. Place your cash near the betting box in front of you and inform the dealer that you would like to get chips. They may be purchased in various denominations so let the dealer know which chips or combination of chips you'd like if you have a particular preference.

To bet, place your chips (or cash) in the betting box directly in front of you. All bets must be placed before the cards are dealt.

WINNING STRATEGIES

There is only one mathematically correct way to play your hand against the dealer. This is called the **Basic Strategy**. The plays shown in the Master Chart in this book form the basis of any winning strategy even for advanced players using card counting and non-card counting strategies.

Keep in mind that many of the plays that should be made are not necessarily winning plays, but instead are plays that minimize your long term losses when you are dealt a bad hand. For example, whenever you are dealt a 16, you've got a hand that will lose more times than not, no matter what the dealer has as an upcard.

However, the strategies here will give you the best chances of beating the casino, and if you follow them, you will be among the top 5% of all blackjack players.

The large number of 10 value cards in the deck has a big effect on the strategies in the game. Combining this information with the knowledge of the dealer's upcard formulates a strategy that makes sense.

When the dealer shows a 4-6 as an upcard, he will bust more than 40% of the time (a little less with a 2 and a 3) and thus you will play more aggressively with your strong hands, doubling and splitting more often. At the same time, you will rarely risk busting, since once you are out of the hand, you lose even if the dealer busts afterwards.

WINNING TIP
Dealer Pat Hands: 7-Ace as Upcard

When the dealer shows a 7, 8, 9, 10 or Ace as an upcard, hit all hard totals of 16 or less. Try to make a total of 17-21 points.

On the other hand, with an upcard of 7 or higher, the dealer will bust only about 25% of the time and make strong hands with his 9, 10 (J, Q, and K), and Ace, and a little less so with his 8. Thus, against these upcards, you play a more conservative game, doubling and splitting less often.

You also draw with the lousy 12-16 hands, risking a bust, since the dealer won't go over 21 that often.

WINNING TIP
Dealer Stiffs: 2-6 as Upcard

Stand on all hard totals of 12 points or more. Do not bust against a dealer's upcard of 2-6. Exception - Hit 12 vs. 2 or 3.

Hitting and Standing

Try to get a 17 or better against the dealer's 7-Ace upcards and don't risk busting against the weak dealer upcards of 2-6 with the exception of hitting 12 against the dealer's upcards of 2 and 3.

On point totals of 11 or less, always draw (if you do not exercise a doubling or splitting option). On point totals of hard 17 or more, stand. There is such a high risk of busting with these hands, it never makes sense to draw.

Doubling

Aggressive doubling down is at the heart of your winning strategy so be sure to make the right plays when they are called for. In general, you'll double down on your 10s and 11s where the draw of a 10 gives you 20s and 21s, and also against the weak dealer upcards of 4, 5 and 6.

Splitting

Splitting is a strategy that allows you to either break up one weak hand into two with better possibilities, or to get more money on the table when you have an advantage.

There are many splitting plays, so study these carefully before going to the tables. In the chart, you'll notice more aggressive plays against the dealer upcards of 2-6, particularly against the 4-6, the weakest of the dealer upcards.

THE MASTER STRATEGY CHART

The following Master Strategy Chart gives you an accurate game against the rules and variations you'll typically play against. The top line represents the dealer's upcard and the left column is the player's hand.

For multiple deck games, make the plays as shown. For single deck games, where there is an asterisk (*) double down, or two asterisks (**), split.

MASTER STRATEGY CHART

- Dealer's Upcard -

	2	3	4	5	6	7	8	9	10	A
7/less	H	H	H	H	H	H	H	H	H	H
8	H	H	H	H*	H*	H	H	H	H	H
9	H*	D	D	D	D	H	H	H	H	H
10	D	D	D	D	D	D	D	D	H	H
11	D	D	D	D	D	D	D	D	D	H*
12	H	H	S	S	S	H	H	H	H	H
13	S	S	S	S	S	H	H	H	H	H
14	S	S	S	S	S	H	H	H	H	H
15	S	S	S	S	S	H	H	H	H	H
16	S	S	S	S	S	H	H	H	H	H
A2	H	H	H*	D	D	H	H	H	H	H
A3	H	H	H*	D	D	H	H	H	H	H
A4	H	H	D	D	D	H	H	H	H	H
A5	H	H	D	D	D	H	H	H	H	H
A6	H*	D	D	D	D	H	H	H	H	H
A7	S	D	D	D	D	S	S	H	H	H
A8	S	S	S	S	S	S	S	S	S	S
A9	S	S	S	S	S	S	S	S	S	S
22	H	H**	spl	spl	spl	spl	H	H	H	H
33	H	H	spl	spl	spl	spl	H	H	H	H
44	H	H	H	H	H	H	H	H	H	H
55	D	D	D	D	D	D	D	D	H	H
66	H**	spl	spl	spl	spl	H	H	H	H	H
77	spl	spl	spl	spl	spl	spl	H	H	H	H
88	spl	spl	spl	spl	spl	spl	spl	spl	spl	spl
99	spl	spl	spl	spl	spl	S	spl	spl	S	S
1010	S	S	S	S	S	S	S	S	S	S
AA	spl	spl	spl	spl	spl	spl	spl	spl	spl	spl

H = Hit   S = Stand   D= Double   spl = Split

*In single deck games, double instead.
**In single deck games, split instead.

3

SEVEN MONEY MANAGEMENT TIPS

TIPS 1-7

Money management is the most important part of the winning formula and is a concept I cannot stress enough. You will see themes relating to this subject interspersed throughout the book and emphasized over and over again. You cannot win without handling your money intelligently, and every gambler, good or bad, lucky or unlucky, knows this to be true.

Follow the advice here carefully because it is the difference between winning and losing, and it is the difference between having a pleasurable if not great gambling experience, or having one that haunts you for years.

One quick tip: Have winning money as a goal–you'll be surprised at the difference in results such a positive attitude might make.

MONEY MANAGEMENT TIP #1

Do not impulsively bet all your remaining chips on one hand.

I should say—never do this. It is simply foolish to impulsively bet all your chips in a win or lose proposition. It defeats the purpose of playing because now it is not about playing strategic blackjack but about the luck of what happens on one bet. If you're winning, all your hard-earned wins can go down the tube in one flash and if you're losing, this is a quick way to make a moderate or bad loss into something much worse. And, if there are just a few chips left, why not just pocket the chips as opposed to trying to get rid of them?

MONEY MANAGEMENT TIP #2

Do not make a ridiculously large bet on one hand.

Just throwing a crazy disproportionate wager to your normal bet size is foolish strategy. It's not even strategy actually, but impulsiveness that will cost you. What do you do if a doubling or splitting situation comes up? Do you dig into your wallet for an even more alarming bet size (and now psychologically commit yourself to more of a table stake that you originally were prepared for) or do you not make the correct aggressive move? If you're tired of playing, just cash out with what you have left. Don't just throw it away.

MONEY MANAGEMENT TIP #3

Do <u>not</u> bet with money you cannot afford to lose - A

This is the single most important concept in the entire book. Forget about winning and losing for a second. Absolutely do not gamble if you cannot afford to take the loss, and that goes not just from a financial point of view, but an emotional point of view as well. Never, under any circumstances whatsoever, put yourself in a compromising situation where rent money, food money, kids money, living money, security money, and whatever else may be important, is put at stake on the blackjack table. Never.

MONEY MANAGEMENT TIP #4

Do <u>not</u> bet with money you cannot afford to lose - B

I'm not done with this discussion, it is far too important. Too many lives are ruined because some fool thinks the tables will change his life. For fools like this, the tables did change their lives, but unfortunately, not in the direction they expected. People get ruined in big ways, and they get ruined in small ways. The house always takes down the desperate people and the greedy people looking for that quick buck–without fail. Be smart, that is what I have to tell you. Play only with money you can afford to lose, both financially and emotionally.

MONEY MANAGEMENT TIP #5

Set loss limits before you sit down at a table.

Winging it on the spot with your bankroll is not a good idea. You need to have goals and loss limits before risking money, because if you don't properly prepare these ideas in a sane environment *away from the table*, you may get caught up in the excitement of the game, and later, when the dust settles, wonder how you could have been so stupid to lose so much money. This is real money, my friend. Having pre-set loss limits are essential to every gambler, no matter the game.

MONEY MANAGEMENT TIP #6

Once you have a good win under your belt, never give it all back.

Protecting your loss limits is crucial, very crucial, but protecting your wins are important as well. Pay attention to this key concept: Once you have won money from the casino, it is yours. Sure, you want to see if you can parlay a win into a big win, and a big win into a monster win, and a monster win into something bigger. All well and good—I'm with you on that. But set half that won money, or even better, two thirds of that money aside, and if the streak rides, keep going; if you fall to your stopgap, walk away with a big smile.

MONEY MANAGEMENT TIP #7

Be smart with your money and keep your emotions under control.

Money management and emotional control are the centerpiece of any winning strategy. All your hard-earned winnings can go to pot in a fit of impulsiveness or loss of emotional control. To be a winner, it is important to always maintain control of your situation and be smart with your money. Minimize you losses with stop-loss limits and protect your wins with fail-safe strategies by using intelligent decision-making on when to quit. The key to any winning strategy in gambling is always based on sound money management. Always.

4

BASIC PLAYING TIPS

TIPS 1-17

In this chapter, we cover 17 basic situations that are not directly related to strategy decisions but which are important for you to know as a blackjack player. We'll look at issues ranging from proper play etiquette and tipping, to the handling of money and betting, to rules that are in place specifically to thwart dishonest players from getting an undue edge.

We cover a wide range of issues that will broaden your knowledge of the game's inner workings, and overall, make you more comfortable at the tables.

Let's move on to tip #1.

BASIC PLAYING TIP #1

Do not hold your cards with two hands.

The proper way to hold cards in blackjack is with *one* hand only. "Why is this?" you might ask. The casinos instituted this policy long ago as a protection against chicanery by players using both hands to switch cards, a much harder feat to accomplish with just one hand. If you do use two hands, the dealer will politely ask you to refrain from using the second hand. Persistent use of two hands could prompt the casino to deny you play.

BASIC PLAYING TIP #2

Do not play out of turn.

The general etiquette of blackjack, and the rules of the game, require that hands are played in turn. Attempting to play your cards out of turn is a red flag that you're a novice to the game. The one exception to this rule is when you have a blackjack in a game where cards are dealt face down. In that situation it is acceptable to turn over the hand as soon as you get it!

BASIC PLAYING TIP #3

Do not mistreat dealers simply because you are having bad luck.

Is it the dealer's fault if you're having a terrible streak of bad luck? Despite many player's feelings to the contrary, winning, losing, what cards you get, and overall luck, good or bad, has nothing to do with the person dealing them. The dealer is just dealing cards–no more. There is a tendency of ill-mannered players to blame dealers for their bad luck and to exhibit rude behavior, such as cursing and card throwing, directed at some unfortunate dealer. Common courtesy mandates that you treat dealers, and people in general, with respect.

BASIC PLAYING TIP #4

When playing with other players, get your bets down in time.

It is a courtesy to other players to have your bets down in time so as not to slow down the game. One of the most annoying things for a blackjack player is to have to wait on some sluggard because he or she can't manage to get their bets down in time. You do this enough times and not only will the dealer be reminding you nicely to get your bet placed, but your fellow players will be doing so in a more hostile manner.

BASIC PLAYING TIP #5

When playing head on with the dealer, play at your own pace.

If you're playing by yourself, head on against the dealer, you can take your sweet time; there are no other players you have to worry about inconveniencing. It's your money, you're the client, and whether the dealer likes it or not, is not your issue. (In fact, if the dealer rushes you, is discourteous, or makes you feel uncomfortable in any manner at all, either change tables, or if you decide to continue playing there, do *not* tip for this bad service.) In any case, the dealer has no place else to go, so take your time and enjoy the game.

BASIC PLAYING TIP #6

Place your bet in the betting circle, not in the area around it.

Blackjack bets belong in the betting circle on the layout as designated by the casino. That is where they are considered a wager. Money placed outside the circle can mean different things; a tip for the dealer, changing chip color (changing one denomination of chips for another) or getting chips for cash. By making bets in areas outside the circle, you create a break in the game's rhythm as the dealer must either move the bet to the betting circle himself, or he must remind you to do it yourself on subsequent plays.

BASIC PLAYING TIP #7

Do not take your cards off the table and out of the dealer's sight!

Taking your cards off the table is a no-no! When cards enter the domain of the player or disappear from the sight line you can imagine what might go on if the wrong types happen to be holding those cards. Obviously, casinos want to protect themselves against this scenario so they have instituted this very sensible rule. Players who remove their cards from the table run the risk of being thrown out of the casino if the pit boss suspects foul play.

BASIC PLAYING TIP #8

Do not tip the dealer when losing, or tip excessively when winning.

Tipping is a courtesy that should be extended for good service and *only* when you're winning. Dealers do not expect tips from players who are losing. You're trying to win money, and if your luck isn't going well, that's just the way it goes. By the same token, if you're winning, don't tip away the profits! I don't know how many times I have seen players tip the dealer every other hand when winning. You can't win money that way! Keep in mind that dealers are on the casino's payroll, not yours, so you don't need to tip if you don't want to.

BASIC PLAYING TIP #9

Indicate your play decisions using hand, not verbal signals.

Due to the many possibilities for confusion with verbal instructions in a noisy casino, and the greater risk of chicanery by voice signals that only players and dealers can interpret, blackjack is played using commonly accepted hand signals: point for a new card, wave your hand to stand and take no more. These hand signals can be verified from the eye in the sky (the security mirrors above the tables) as well as pit bosses where verbal instructions are not as verifiable.

BASIC PLAYING TIP #10

Make sure to tip the waitress when she brings you a drink.

Getting served drinks at the table is just like getting served drinks at a bar; tipping is customary and expected. Most players tip 50¢ or $1 per drink order, or if multiple drinks come in the order (perhaps you're ordering for some friends as well), perhaps even a few dollars might be appropriate.

BASIC PLAYING TIP #11

Play to have a good time! Don't ignore this important rule.

Make sure that you are having fun at blackjack, or at the very least, even though you maybe be losing, feeling somewhat okay during the playing session. How many times have we all seen miserable players at the table, seemingly grinding it out hour after hour or, even worse, losing badly and being unhappy? Don't let that happen to you! If the game is no longer fun, stop playing. Why do something you are not having fun at? *Really*. This is serious advice that unfortunately, most players ignore. Either have fun or don't play!

BASIC PLAYING TIP #12

Practice and study up on your strategies before playing.

I've earned my money through hard work and I'm not about to give the casino any advantage I don't have to. Why should you? With a little effort, even a few hours, you can greatly improve your game and give yourself the best possible chances of winning. The important basic strategies that will make you an excellent player are in this book. Learn them. If you're serious enough and want to have an actual edge over the casino, you should learn the advanced counting or non-counting strategies we advertise in the back of the book.

BASIC PLAYING TIP #13

Neatly stack the chips you are betting with into one even pile.

Casinos like their games to run smoothly and efficiently. Stacking chips evenly allows for faster, more mistake-free payoffs. Before dealing out the cards, a well-trained dealer will always straighten out the betting stacks. If your chips are already neat, it will help the game run more smoothly.

BASIC PLAYING TIP #14

Make sure you receive the proper payoffs on your bets. Pay attention!

Dealers almost always get the payoffs right, but they do make mistakes, just like anyone else, and you don't want that mistake to be at your expense. Most of the time, verification of the proper payoff is easy. The dealer matches up the original bet with an equal number of chips of the same color. Pay more attention to doubling and splitting payouts on blackjacks and when your bet includes mixed denominations. You should no sooner walk away from a bank window without counting your money as you should not verify a proper payoff.

BASIC PLAYING TIP #15

Do not give unsolicited advice to other gamblers at the table.

It is not a good idea to advise players on the best way to play a hand if they haven't asked for such advice. While your advice might be correct in the best way to play a hand, it doesn't mean it will work that *particular* time. Blackjack is a game of percentages and while you may understand that, other players may not. You don't want to be blamed for someone else's ill-fated result. Worry about your own cards, there is enough to keep you busy there.

BASIC PLAYING TIP #16

Tip the dealer by making a separate bet for him or her above your bet.

It is customary in blackjack to tip a dealer by making a bet for him or her on your hand as opposed to actually tipping outright. While the latter is certainly acceptable, the preferred way among experienced players is to place the tip a few inches above the betting circle (toward the dealer) when you make a bet for your own hand. This is commonly understood to be a bet for the dealer. If you win, the bet for the dealer is won as well and gives the dealer double the tip, which they certainly appreciate.

BASIC PLAYING TIP #17

Change your cash into chips at the table.

Chips are received at the table in exchange for cash. This is standard operating procedure in a casino. Just give the dealer whatever cash you want exchanged into chips and he will give you the equivalent number of chips in return. Cashing out, on the other hand, is done at a cashier's cage, and not at the table itself.

5

GENERAL
WINNING TIPS

TIPS 1-15

In this chapter is a collection of general winning tips and strategies that are essential to your success as a blackjack player. We don't actually look at specific strategy plays here, those are covered in the Play-by-Play chapters, rather we'll examine the essential aspects of the game that have so much else to do with winning and losing; how to deal with annoying players, how to choose profitable games, how to mentally prepare yourself to have winning sessions, and overall, how to get into that winning frame of mind.

We've chosen 15 strategic and money-making concepts and situations for this discussion. We'll start, of course, with General Winning Tip #1.

GENERAL WINNING TIP #1

Play single deck over multiple deck if the opportunity exists.

Single deck is an inherently more favorable game for you than the multiple deck by about one half percent. This is essentially due to the greater volatility of cards in the smaller deck. However, you won't often get that option as multiple deck blackjack has become the predominant style of play in casinos. Multiple deck blackjack is still a good game, but even there, with all else being equal, choose two decks over four decks, and four decks over six decks.

GENERAL WINNING TIP #2

Choose games that offer you the best rules and variations.

Blackjack is a game of small percentages and every time you can get some kind of small edge, grab it! If you have a choice, for example in Las Vegas where there are lots of casinos competing against each other for your gambling dollars, look for the games that offer the best rules and options. One casino may perhaps offer doubling allowed after splitting, another may offer surrender, or maybe even resplitting Aces. With all else equal, why not play with the better rules and percentages?

GENERAL WINNING TIP #3

Learn the Basic Strategy to give yourself the best chance of winning!

Winning is what it is all about, but to give yourself the best chance of winning, you need to learn the proper plays for all the situations you might face at the game. In this book, I have provided you with a Master Chart for all the correct Basic Strategies and every type of situation in a question and discussion format to get you ready. Blackjack is a game of percentages. There is only one mathematically correct play for every situation. This is commonly called Basic Strategy. Learn it.

GENERAL WINNING TIP #4

Make the proper play all the time! Do not play hunches.

Leave your hunches at home! They have no place in blackjack, which is essentially a mathematical game. Your hunches and feelings and guesses won't change your luck for the better as you would like to think. They will work against you every time they cause you to deviate from the best percentage play. In the short run, hunches will work out now and then, but in the long run, you'll be giving up percentage points and essentially, giving away money.

GENERAL WINNING TIP #5

Do not play gimmick blackjack games that really are hustles.

Casinos are always looking for that extra edge, some way to get more play at their tables. You'll periodically see "gimmick" blackjack games offered, which on the surface sound great, but when you dig into them, find out that they ultimately are to your disadvantage. For example, while one variation may allow doubling down on any number of cards, as compensation for the house, only even money might be paid on blackjacks, not 3-2, which costs you about 2.5%! The extra doubling situations are nice, but not at the cost of a 2.5% loss!

GENERAL WINNING TIP #6

Do not sit at the same table as players who annoy you.

Casinos are loaded with annoying people and unfortunately, they sometimes happen to be playing at your table and annoying you. You could be annoyed by their style of play, their personality might be too loud or obnoxious, they might be a general nuisance, or they might just make bad plays that seem to cause your big hands to lose. Whether you play blackjack for fun or for profit, you still want to win when playing for fun and you still want to have fun when playing to win. There's a very easy solution for this: change tables.

GENERAL WINNING TIP #7

Do not play at a table where you don't like the dealer.

What goes for playing with annoying players goes for playing with dealers you don't like: you'll end up being more preoccupied with the dealer than with making the correct plays and this will cost you money. And, equally important, you certainly won't be having fun. The advice here is simple, very simple: don't play in any situation you are not comfortable being in, whether it is due to a fellow player or to a dealer that annoys you. This is very straightforward advice, but too often, players ignore this sensible concept until it is too late.

GENERAL WINNING TIP #8

Do not play when you're under the influence.

It's no secret: alcohol and drugs impair decision-making and this will cost you money in blackjack. I have one hard and fast piece of advice for every blackjack player and it takes on all sorts of meanings with the same goal, regardless of circumstance. Never give the house any more of an advantage than you have to. I believe in winning, and anything that takes you away from winning is not good. That includes playing when you can't concentrate, that includes hunch-playing, and that includes playing drunk or being woozy from drugs.

GENERAL WINNING TIP #9

Play blackjack with the goal of winning foremost in your mind.

Play to be a winner! This is not just fluffy advice, your attitude at the table really makes a difference in the way you end up playing. This may sound strange, but I think you'll know this to be true: many players play to lose. You see them every day in the casinos playing so poorly or recklessly that no other result but losing will pry them away from the tables. Don't be one of them. Prepare yourself, think positive about what you need to do, and then go out there and win!

GENERAL WINNING TIP #10

When formulating strategy, assume the dealer's downcard is a 10.

Ten value cards (the Ten, Jack, Queen, and King) form almost 1/3 of the deck of cards and are four times more likely to be held than any other card value. When we add nines to this group and figure that two card dealer draws will sometimes add up to 9 or 10 (or 11 points also), such as a 6 and a 4, we see that this type of theoretical thinking actually makes sense. And from a strategic point of view, it almost always makes sense.

GENERAL WINNING TIP #11

Do not play blackjack if you're afraid to make the aggressive move

As I have tried to stress throughout this book, blackjack is a game of small percentages, and you need to use everything at your disposal to even out the odds and then bring them into your favor. However, if you are afraid to make the aggressive doubling down or splitting plays as called for in the Basic Strategy, then either you are betting over your head or you need to get committed to understanding why aggressive plays are made and how important they are to a winning strategy.

GENERAL WINNING TIP #12

Always prepare for a real game by studying the Basic Strategies first.

If you're getting ready to play blackjack for real money in a casino, prepare yourself first by going over all the Basic Strategy plays: hitting and standing, hard and soft doubling, splitting, and the general concepts of strategy *and* money management. Don't get lazy! You want to play with confidence and the skills of winning. To be a winning player, you should be comfortable with the strategies, so take those few minutes to refamiliarize yourself with whatever strategies you need brushing up on. Then go out there and win!

GENERAL WINNING TIP #13

Always be in control of your game and be smart with your money.

The key to any winning strategy in gambling is always based on sound money management. Always. This is so important that I will reiterate the same principle as stressed in Money Management Concept #7. To be a winner, you must always be in control of your situation and be smart with your money. Winners always have one thing in common–they can handle losing. Winners never allow themselves to get beat too bad in any one session, and when winning, make sure they walk away a winner. Learn from that thinking.

GENERAL WINNING TIP #14

Do not take playing or betting advice from other players

There is a world full of losers in casinos and few, if any, know what they are doing. These players are not the people to take advice from, not unless you want to join their ranks. And don't be impressed by "old-timers" who have been hacking away at the game for decades. Experience in blackjack doesn't equate to knowledge as it might in other pursuits. In blackjack, knowledge is *only* acquired through study. The information in this book or in any other Cardoza publication contains the strategies you need to know to be a winner.

GENERAL WINNING TIP #15

If you're a serious player, learn the advanced winning strategies.

You can make money playing blackjack–with the odds, but it requires first, that you know the Basic Strategies, as they are the basis for any winning plan, and second, that you learn a counting or non-counting strategy. Players find that the Cardoza card counting strategies are surprisingly easy (they were designed for use under actual casino conditions), but for those who feel intimidated by the imposing concept of "card counting," we developed the Multiple Deck Non-Counter, which gives players the edge without counting cards.

6

PLAY BY PLAY
HITTING & STANDING

SITUATIONS 1-9

This section looks at the basic hitting and standing decisions you'll face at the blackjack table. These are the bread and butter plays you will encounter more than any of the other situations.

There are really two basic situations in the hitting and standing strategies; when the dealer has a 7, 8, 9, 10 or Ace as an upcard, and thus, will not bust often; and when the dealer has a 2, 3, 4, 5 or 6 as an upcard, and will bust frequently. The dealer's bust frequency is our first consideration when deciding how to play our cards, then of course, we have to see the cards we hold in relation to the dealer's total.

In general, when the dealer has a high likelihood of making a 17 or better, we try to achieve 17 or better ourselves, and when the dealer has a higher likelihood of busting, we try not to bust ourselves.

Nine situations to test your skills against. The challenge is on, see how you do!

SITUATION #1

You're dealt a hard 12 and the dealer has a 2 for an upcard. What is the correct play?

Example Hand

YOU HAVE   **DEALER**

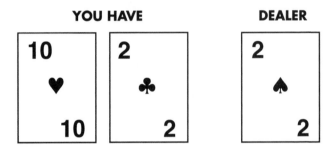

THE RIGHT PLAY TO MAKE

Draw! Don't feel bad if you didn't correctly get this answer. It is a difficult play that players often get wrong. Hitting 12 versus the 2 is an exception to a general rule in blackjack that we will cover in the next few situations. Essentially, with fewer cards to bust our 12 (only the ten value cards, not the 9s or any lower values will bust the 12), and fewer cards to bust the dealer's total, the correct play is to try to improve by drawing.

Draw 12 against the dealer's upcards of 2 *and* 3, but against the 4, 5 and 6, be sure to stand.

Did You Get it Right?   Yes! ☐   No ☐

SITUATION #2

You have a *hard* total of 12 and the dealer's upcard is a 4. Hit or stand?

Example Hand

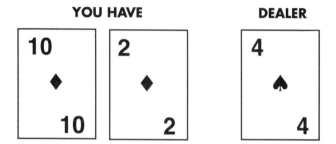

YOU HAVE		DEALER
10 ♦ 10	2 ♦ 2	4 ♠ 4

THE RIGHT PLAY TO MAKE

Stand! Once we go over 21 and bust our hand, we automatically lose, regardless of whether the dealer busts as well afterwards. This is our biggest disadvantage in blackjack. But we have a big advantage as well. While the dealer must draw to 16 or less and stand on 17 or better, we can hit or stand (or use our other options) in the ways it most benefits our hand. So when we know that the dealer has a high chance of busting, in other words, the dealer is sitting there with a 2, 3, 4, 5 or 6 as an upcard, than we do not risk busting our *hard* totals of 12-16. (Exception: Hit 12 against the dealer's 2 or 3 as we discussed previously.)

Did You Get it Right?   Yes! ☐   No ☐

SITUATION #3

You have a *hard* total of 13 the dealer's upcard is a 5. Hit or stand?

Example Hand

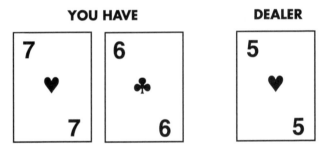

YOU HAVE   **DEALER**

THE RIGHT PLAY TO MAKE

Stand. This play is so important, that I wanted to present another situation to drive this point home. One of the cardinal rules in blackjack is to stand when the dealer has a busting situation, that is, he holds upcards of 2-6. If we draw and bust, it doesn't matter that the dealer may bust after–our money will already have been collected, and we've lost the hand. This play should be second nature to you as a blackjack player. If it isn't, you need to spend more time preparing for the tables. With any hard total of 12-16, stand if the dealer has a busting card, a 2, 3, 4, 5 or 6 showing as an upcard, with the exception of 12 vs. 2 or 3, where it's a draw.

Did You Get it Right?   Yes! ☐   No ☐

SITUATION #4

You have a *hard* total of 13 against a dealer upcard of 10. What's the correct play?

Example Hand

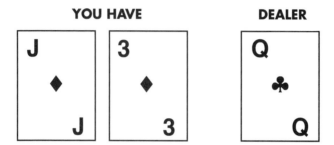

YOU HAVE   **DEALER**

THE RIGHT PLAY TO MAKE

Draw. The thinking is simple here. The dealer is most likely to make a hand. We assume a possible ten value card in the hole for a dealer pat hand, as we discussed earlier, which means that if we don't draw to improve, we automatically lose in these situations–about 75% of the time! The hand is terrible, but we don't want to go down without fighting. Sitting there hoping the dealer will bust is worse than drawing and risking the bust ourselves. This play is an example of minimizing losses.

With any hard total of 12-16, we must draw if the dealer has a 7, 8, 9, 10 or Ace.

Did You Get it Right?   Yes! ☐   No ☐

SITUATION #5

You have a *hard* total of 16 the dealer has a 10. Stand or draw?

Example Hand

YOU HAVE	DEALER

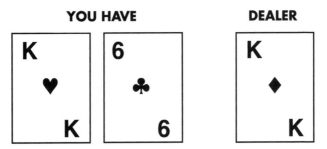

DRAW **THE RIGHT PLAY TO MAKE**

~~Stand.~~ While 16 versus 10 is a very close play, it is still better to draw than stand. "But," you say, "I seem to bust all the time when I draw." It is true, we will bust often, as the drawing of any of the eight out of the 13 ranks, the 6 through the Ace, will put us out of business. What can you do though? We're dealt a bad hand and we have to make the best of it. While the prospects of hitting 16 vs. 10 are not good, the play is a gain over standing, a minimize loss strategy that is so necessary in blackjack.

With a hard total of 12-16, draw vs. 7, 8, 9, 10, Ace.

Did You Get it Right?   Yes! ☐   No ☐

SITUATION #6

You have **9 points (or less)** and the dealer shows a pat card, **7, 8, 9, 10 or Ace.** When might you stand?

Example Hand

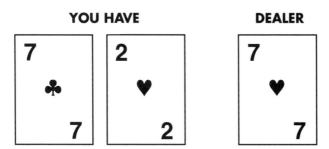

YOU HAVE	DEALER
7♣ 7 2♥ 2	7♥ 7

THE RIGHT PLAY TO MAKE

The answer is never! Always draw (if not double or split) with 11 points or less. It doesn't matter what the dealer has as an upcard; standing on 11 points or less would be among the worst plays possible in blackjack. (There are some other terrible moves as well but this play would rank up there among the worst ones.)

Drawing can only improve what you have; in fact it's impossible to make the hand any worse. With 11 points or less, the only way to win is if the dealer busts, but why not try to improve your hand when there is no risk at all?

Did You Get it Right?   Yes! ☐   No ☐

SITUATION #7

You have 9 points (or less) and the dealer shows a bust card, 2, 3, 4, 5 or 6. Do you always draw?

Example Hand

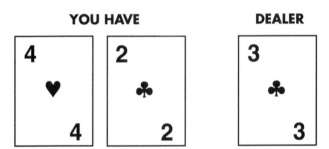

YOU HAVE   **DEALER**

THE RIGHT PLAY TO MAKE

Except for the times you have a doubling or splitting play, you should always draw. Less than 9 points, or for that matter, less than 11 points is always a draw situation. Only a complete fool will stand with a hand that can only improve and has no risk of busting.

Always analyze a hand first for doubling or splitting possibilities, and if they are not present *and* favorable, then see if it's a draw or stand that is appropriate to the situation. However, never, ever stand on any total of less than 11 points.

Did You Get it Right? Yes! ☐ No ☐

SITUATION #8

You have a hard total of 16 and the dealer has a 10 or Ace showing. What's your play?

Example Hand

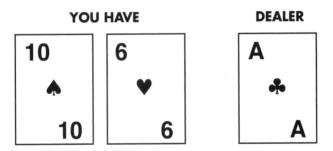

YOU HAVE		DEALER
10 ♠ 10	6 ♥ 6	A ♣ A

THE RIGHT PLAY TO MAKE

Draw—always draw. We already talked about trying to make a hand of 17 or better when the dealer has an upcard of 7 or higher, but I see this play made so often, it is worth making this hand a discussion by itself.

Players are tempted to stand on 16s against a 10 or Ace because they bust so often drawing on them. Holding a 16 against the dealer's 10 or ace is a terrible percentage situation where you'll lose about three out of four times. However, in the long term, while you'll still lose badly, you'll lose less, because there is a gain by drawing over standing.

Did You Get it Right?   Yes! ☐   No ☐

SITUATION #9

You have a total comprised of three cards. Do you play your hands differently than the same two card total?

Example Hand

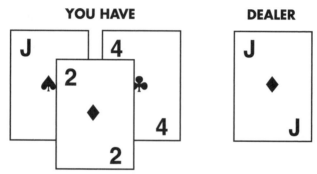

YOU HAVE   **DEALER**

THE RIGHT PLAY TO MAKE

I often get asked how to play three card 16s or three card 12s in certain situations, and the answer I invariably give is this: make the same play with three cards as you would if you had two cards. This also holds for four and even five card hands as well.

With the exception of doubling down or splitting situations, which don't apply on three or more card hands anyway, what is correct for two card play is correct for three cards or more. Thus, no, you don't play three card hands differently than 2 card ones.

Did You Get it Right?   Yes! ☐   No ☐

7

PLAY BY PLAY
HARD DOUBLING

SITUATIONS 10-22

Doubling down is our biggest offensive weapon and it must be used wisely to get the maximum advantage against the casino. It is a favorable player option that must be used aggressively when the Basic Strategy calls for doubling down so that we can offset the disadvantage of having to act first on our hands. Therefore, it is important to learn the proper times to double down and to follow through by always making the plays.

We have 13 hands in this section to challenge you, with a variety of basic and tricky doubling situations in the mix.

See how well you score on the hard doubling plays.

SITUATION #10

You may have a good double down or split but can't remember the correct play. What should you do?

Example Hand

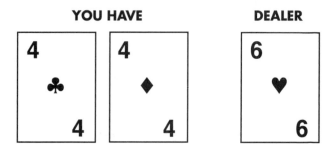

YOU HAVE		DEALER

THE RIGHT PLAY TO MAKE

Leave the table! You should take a break and refamiliarize yourself with the proper doubling and splitting strategies. Players that don't make the correct plays cannot consistently beat the casino at blackjack. To be a winner, you must be prepared and be fully conversant with the correct basic strategies.

By the way, the correct play above depend upon the rules and number of decks being played. The hand of 44 versus 6 is a draw in a multiple deck game, a double down if the game was single deck, and a split if the game allowed doubling after splitting!

Did You Get it Right?   Yes! ☐   No ☐

SITUATION #11

You are dealt an 11 against a dealer 10 in a <u>multiple</u> deck game. Should you double down here?

Example Hand

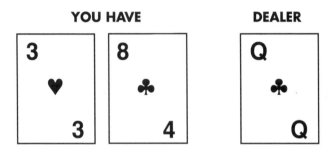

YOU HAVE   **DEALER**

THE RIGHT PLAY TO MAKE

Absolutely! When you get dealt an 11, let that bring a smile to your face because you have a great hand. Indeed! Against every card but the Ace in a multiple deck game, you have a huge doubling advantage over the casino. Any of the four ten value cards will give you a 21, which of course, is impossible to beat. A 9 will give you a 20, and an 8 will give you a 19, two more really strong hands that will put in an advantageous position at double your money.

Don't miss the opportunity to make more money with these plays.

Did You Get it Right?   Yes! ☐   No ☐

SITUATION #12

You are dealt an 11 and the dealer shows an Ace in a <u>single</u> deck game. Is doubling down correct?

Example Hand

YOU HAVE   **DEALER**

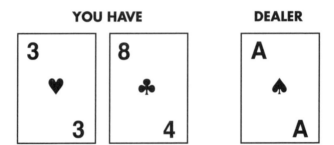

THE RIGHT PLAY TO MAKE

Again, this is the correct play in a single deck game. Even though the dealer has the powerful Ace, which doesn't bust often, our 11 is even stronger since a 10 to our 11 is unbeatable. We already know the dealer doesn't have a 21 or he would have turned over a blackjack already.

Doubling 10 against an Ace in a single deck game should always be made.

Did You Get it Right?   Yes! ☐   No ☐

SITUATION #13

You are dealt an 11 and the dealer shows an Ace in a <u>multiple</u> deck game. Is doubling down correct?

Example Hand

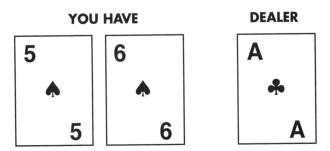

YOU HAVE		DEALER

THE RIGHT PLAY TO MAKE

No, it is not correct to double down an 11 against an Ace in a multiple deck game. In fact, the dealer's Ace is the only upcard we will *not* double down against in a multiple deck game. (In single deck games, you double down with 11 no matter what upcard the dealer holds.) The lack of sensitivity to particular card removal in multiple deck games is what separates the strategy from single deck play.

We have a profitable situation, but not quite profitable enough to give up our option to draw again if our card is weak.

Did You Get it Right? Yes! ☐   No ☐

SITUATION #14

You are dealt a 10 and the dealer's upcard is a 9. Is it correct to hit or double down?

Example Hand

YOU HAVE   **DEALER**

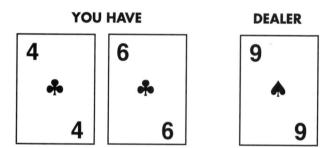

THE RIGHT PLAY TO MAKE

Doubling down is the right play not only against the 9, but against every card weaker than that, the 2-8 as well. Doubling down with 10 points against weaker dealer upcards is a major asset in your doubling repertoire and will account for lots of money in your pile.

If we draw a 10 for a total of 20, we will most likely win–at double the money! A hand of 20 beats a 19 every day of the week. Sometimes we won't draw that 10 but neither will the dealer, so we may still be okay, but when we do draw the 10, we have a strong hand that can weather strong dealer draws.

Did You Get it Right?   Yes! ☐   No ☐

SITUATION #15

You are dealt a 9 and the dealer shows a 4. Do you simply draw a card or do you double down?

Example Hand

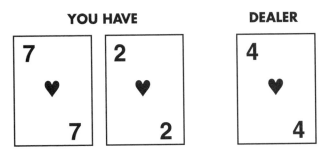

YOU HAVE   **DEALER**

THE RIGHT PLAY TO MAKE

This is a double down situation we want to take advantage of. With the many 10 value cards in the deck, we hope to make a 19, which is a very strong total. Drawing a 9 brings our hand to an 18, which is respectable, or an 8, to a 17, which is weak but better than a 16 or less. An Ace draw would give us a powerful 20. Any other cards we might draw are bad and would require the dealer to bust for us to win. But he'll do that often with those weak dealer upcards.

With our starting total of 9 and this type of outlook, we will take advantage of the weak dealer bust cards.

Did You Get it Right?   Yes! ☐   No ☐

SITUATION #16

It's a <u>multiple</u> deck game. You have 9 points and the dealer shows a 2. Hit or double down?

Example Hand

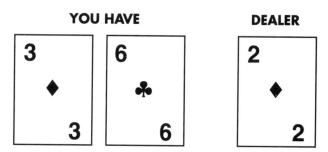

YOU HAVE   **DEALER**

THE RIGHT PLAY TO MAKE

Do not double down. This time, the correct play is to draw only. The dealer makes too many hands with a 2–in fact he will draw an 18 or better more than half the time–to make this a profitable double down in a multiple deck game. It is correct to double down in a multiple deck game against the dealer's 3-6 only.

Note that in a single deck game, due to the lesser number of cards in the deck and the sensitivity to particular card removal, this is a correct double down in the basic strategy.

Did You Get it Right?   Yes! ☐   No ☐

SITUATION #17

The dealer's upcard is a 7. You're thinking about doubling with 9 points. Do you do it?

Example Hand

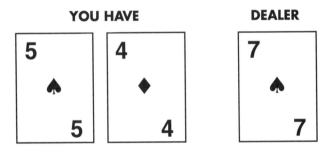

YOU HAVE		DEALER
5 ♠ 5	4 ♦ 4	7 ♠ 7

THE RIGHT PLAY TO MAKE

No, you don't–hit only. While the 9 is a great starting total that will make lots of very strong 19s, giving up the option to draw again should we get a poor draw and not a 10 value card is not profitable against an upcard the dealer will make lots of hands with.

Don't misunderstand; we have a clear advantage against the dealer's 7, and if we draw a 10, we're in like Flint. We'll win big overall with a 19 vs. a 7. But the times we don't get that magic 10 will cost us too much for all the 17s or better the dealer will make. We'll win plenty here, but not enough to justify doubling.

Did You Get it Right?   Yes! ☐   No ☐

SITUATION #18

Again we hold a 9 against the dealer's 7, but this time it's a <u>single</u> deck game. Do you double now?

Example Hand

YOU HAVE **DEALER**

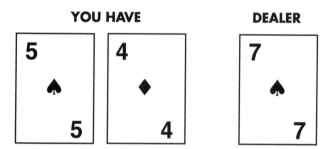

THE RIGHT PLAY TO MAKE

No again. It is never correct to double down with a 9 against any dealer pat card–cards of 7 through Ace that will make 17s or better for the dealer more than 75% of the time. We have a great starting total, but if that 10 doesn't show up, we're sitting ducks at double the money.

Holding 9 vs. 7 is a hand we would like to see all day long–it's very profitable. However, the correct play is to simply draw in a single or multiple deck game. It is only correct to double with 9 points against the dealer's 3-6 in a multiple deck game, or 2-6 in a single deck one.

Did You Get it Right?   Yes! ☐   No ☐

SITUATION #19

It's a __multiple__ deck game, the dealer is sitting with a very weak 6 and we hold 8 points. Hit or double down?

Example Hand

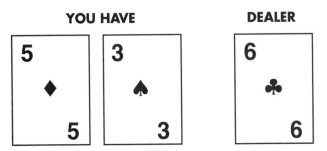

YOU HAVE

DEALER

THE RIGHT PLAY TO MAKE

Doubling with 8 points against *any* dealer upcard is a no-no in multiple deck games. The potential 18 is simply not strong enough to risk doubling the money and giving up the option to draw an additional card if the first one is a bad draw.

Against the dealer bust cards, you simply don't have enough upside potential to weather the times when the dealer does draw out to a 17 or better and we're sitting there with dead hands that can use one more draw.

(Note: In a single deck game, it is correct to double 8 vs. 5 or 6.)

Did You Get it Right?   Yes! ☐   No ☐

SITUATION #20

We're playing a <u>single</u> deck game, same situation, our 8 vs. a 6. Hit or double down?

Example Hand

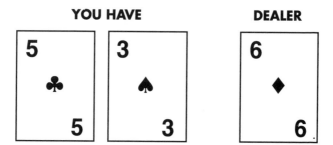

YOU HAVE   **DEALER**

THE RIGHT PLAY TO MAKE

Double down! In a single deck game, the double down is correct against not only the dealer's 5, but the 6 as well. Look at the cards in the example. Not only are those three cards we don't want to draw on our 8 and can't because they are out of play but they are three cards we don't want to see the dealer draw either—or hold as downcards.

The effect of this small card removal in from a pack of only 52 cards makes 8 vs. 5 or 6 a correct double down in single deck play (but not multiple deck).

Did You Get it Right?   Yes! ☐   No ☐

SITUATION #21

The dealer appears to be a sitting duck with an upcard of 6. We have 7 points. Hit or double down?

Example Hand

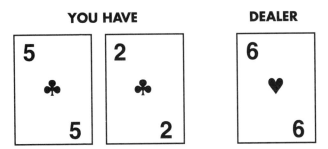

YOU HAVE		DEALER
5 ♣ 5	2 ♣ 2	6 ♥ 6

THE RIGHT PLAY TO MAKE

Always hit, <u>never</u> double. Don't even think about it. Unless you know the dealer will bust, and I don't know how you would ever know that, never, ever double down with 7 points or less. There is no two ways about this play. With 7 points, any way you shake it, it's a clear draw.

Did You Get it Right?   Yes! ☐   No ☐

SITUATION #22

It's a <u>single</u> deck game. You hold 7 points and just *know* the dealer will bust. Should you double down?

Example Hand

YOU HAVE   **DEALER**

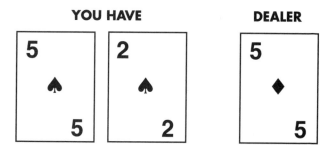

THE RIGHT PLAY TO MAKE

What? Never double here. Unless all the cards were open or you could read the future, you have to be lacking some serious connections in the cranial anatomy to even think of doubling down on this hand.

At best, a 10 will give you a lousy 17 which will beat virtually nothing in this game. Sure, you'll win when the dealer busts, but no matter what the dealer holds as an upcard, even the 6, he will make more hands than bust, and you will be out at double your money. That would be pretty foolish.

Did You Get it Right?   Yes! ☐   No ☐

8

PLAY BY PLAY SOFT DOUBLING

SITUATIONS 23-41

Doubling down on soft totals, hands where you hold an Ace that can be counted as 1 point or 11, are plays made by savvy players who want to get every advantage out of the favorable situations offered. Some players never quite get what soft doubling is about, and as a result, they pass up key times when they can increase their bets in advantageous situations.

As we've seen before, we get more aggressive with our soft doubling against the weak dealer upcards that bust the most, the 4, 5 and 6, and at the same time, play more carefully against the tricky three and the dangerous deuce.

One concept to keep in mind: never double down with a soft total if the dealer holds a 7, 8, 9, 10 or Ace as an upcard. That would be suicide.

Let's see how well you can do in soft doubling situations.

SITUATION #23

You hold an Ace and a 7, 18 points, and the dealer has a 10. What's the correct play?

Example Hand

YOU HAVE　　　　　　　　**DEALER**

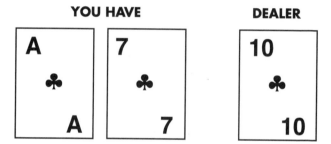

THE RIGHT PLAY TO MAKE

Drawing is the right play! A total of 18 is only a fair hand, no better than that, and against the powerful 10, it is not even a fair total but a weak total. You need to play for a better shot and the soft nature of the hand gives you that opportunity.

You're against the eight ball here and have to make a move. You'll often grab 10s and will be no better off. However, you'll be surprised at the number of times you get dealt an Ace, 2, or 3, and will beat the dealer or even draw a second time after a weak draw to improve. In any case, correct strategy dictates drawing.

Did You Get it Right?　　Yes! ☐　　　　No ☐

SITUATION #24

It's __single__ deck, you hold an Ace and a 7, and the dealer has an Ace. What's the correct play?

Example Hand

YOU HAVE **DEALER**

THE RIGHT PLAY TO MAKE

Hit! It doesn't matter whether you're playing in a single deck game or a multiple deck one—the strategy is the same. For all intents and purposes, the dealer may just as well have a 10 or a 9 as an upcard. We're at a big disadvantage against these strong upcards, and the flexibility of the soft total gives us a chance to improve. Keep in mind that an 18 is not a strong hand as many players think, it is only fair, so drawing here is not risking the ruination of a good hand, especially vs. an Ace.

Whenever you hold a soft 18 (of two cards or more), you should draw against the dealer's 9, 10 and Ace.

Did You Get it Right?   Yes! ☐   No ☐

SITUATION #25

We have A7, a soft 18, and the dealer has a 7. Draw, double, stand?

Example Hand

YOU HAVE   **DEALER**

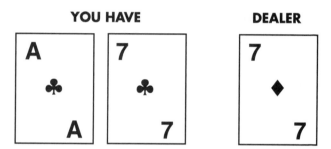

THE RIGHT PLAY TO MAKE

You're in good shape now, stand! Your 18 puts you in the driver's seat against that weaker dealer 7. In fact, it is too bad you couldn't be dealt that situation all day long. You would get rich quick.

Soft 18 against the dealer's 7 is clearly not a double down (only hands of 10 and 11 would be correct doubles against the dealer's 7), and drawing would simply be foolish. Always tand with soft 18 vs. the dealer's 7.

Did You Get it Right?   Yes! ☐   No ☐

SITUATION #26

We have A7, a soft 18, and this time the dealer has an 8. Draw, double, stand?

Example Hand

YOU HAVE	DEALER

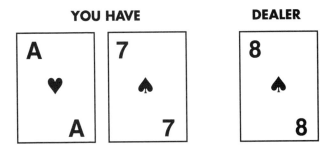

THE RIGHT PLAY TO MAKE

Stand! Your 18 against the dealer's potential 18 puts you in a reasonably strong place and you certainly don't want to risk a weaker total. There will be a lot of pushes here, and when not, the dealer will be drawing in situations where he or she can bust.

Doubling or drawing are out of the question. This is a clear stand.

Did You Get it Right?　Yes! ☐　　　No ☐

SITUATION #27

We have a soft 18, and the dealer's upcard is a 4. Draw, double, stand?

Example Hand

YOU HAVE   **DEALER**

THE RIGHT PLAY TO MAKE

Double down, my friend. Against the 4, as well as the 5 and 6, the highest dealer busting cards, we take advantage of our doubling power and lay more money down.

Any ten value card gives us back the same 18–but with double the money–while Aces, 2s, and 3s give us an even better hand, again with double the bet. All good stuff. And when we don't draw well, the dealer will bust more than 40% of the time starting with those 4-6s.

Did You Get it Right?   Yes! ☐   No ☐

SITUATION #28

We have a soft 18, and the dealer's upcard is the versatile 3. Draw, double, stand?

Example Hand

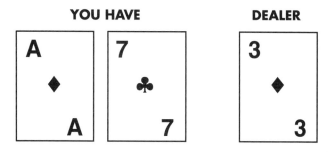

| YOU HAVE | DEALER |

THE RIGHT PLAY TO MAKE

What to do? Double down! We sit with a hand holding all sorts of possibilities. Drawing a 10 gives us a reasonably strong 18 vs. the dealer's 3, and draws of an Ace, 2 and 3 make us even stronger. At the same time, while the dealer won't bust as often as with the 4, 5, and 6, he'll still be busting plenty.

Doubling in this situation is an excellent play made by good players.

Did You Get it Right?   Yes! [ ]   No [ ]

SITUATION #29

We have a soft 18, and the dealer's upcard is the tricky 2. Draw, double, stand?

Example Hand

YOU HAVE		DEALER

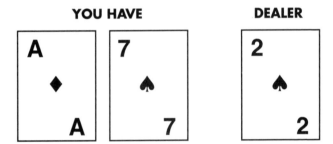

THE RIGHT PLAY TO MAKE

Do not draw or double down with an A7 against the dealer's 2–stand! The dealer's 2 makes far too many hands for us to get aggressive in this situation. In fact, starting with a 2, the dealer will make an 18 or better more than half the time. You don't want double your money on the table nor do you want to weaken that 18 which can hold its own here.

There is not enough dealer busting potential as with the 3, or for that matter, the 4, 5, and 6 to make this a correct double. Thus, with soft 18 vs. 2, stand.

Did You Get it Right?   Yes! ☐   No ☐

SITUATION #30

We hold soft 17, the dealer shows an 8 as an upcard. Is this a draw situation?

Example Hand

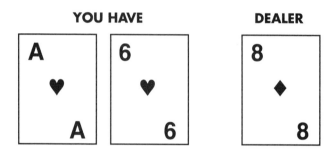

YOU HAVE

A ♥ A   6 ♥ 6

DEALER

8 ♦ 8

THE RIGHT PLAY TO MAKE

It's absolutely a draw situation! You're not sitting pretty with a 17 against a potential 18, not at all. Nor are you any better off if the dealer shows a 9, 10, or Ace as an upcard. In fact, you're in even worse shape. Even a draw of a 9 for 16 points doesn't make you much worse off in these situations and the 10s keep things status quo. However, Aces, 2s, 3s, and 4s considerably change the outlook for the better.

It's a cardinal rule in blackjack: never stand on a soft 17. If you don't have a double, you should draw.

Did You Get it Right? Yes! ☐   No ☐

SITUATION #31

We hold soft 17 against the dealer's upcard of 7, a potential push. Stand, draw or even double?

Example Hand

YOU HAVE **DEALER**

THE RIGHT PLAY TO MAKE

Draw! Do not stand ever on Ace-6, not today, not tomorrow, not even when the cows come home or the moon is blue. Never, ever. The hand of 17 stinks. If you were dealt a 17 hand after hand, you would lose a fortune, and quickly. When you are dealt a hard 17, there is not much you can do. However, when the 17 is soft, no card will possibly bust your hand and you have many opportunities to improve.

Doubling against a 7? I don't think so. Stand? Nope. Draw soft 17 vs. a 7.

Did You Get it Right?   Yes! ☐   No ☐

SITUATION #32

We hold soft 17 and the dealer has the weak 6 as an upcard. This looks like a double down. Is it?

Example Hand

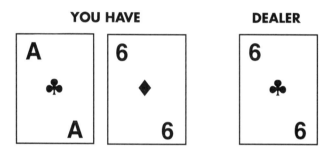

YOU HAVE   **DEALER**

THE RIGHT PLAY TO MAKE

Yes it is! Double down. The dealer is weak and will bust often with the 6. We will also take advantage of the other weak dealer upcards, the 4 and 5, cards which will bust more than 40% for the dealer. When he doesn't bust, we will also be making hands. The tens don't do much but they do give us a little value, while Aces, 2s, 3s, and 4s give us hands that are favorites to win, if not better.

Doubling down is a big asset to the astute player and you want to take advantage of it every profitable opportunity you can.

Did You Get it Right?   Yes! ☐   No ☐

SITUATION #33

We hold soft 17 and the dealer flips over the 3 for an upcard. Stand, double, draw?

Example Hand

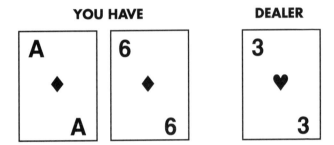

YOU HAVE		DEALER

THE RIGHT PLAY TO MAKE

Double down! As we discussed earlier, you'll never stand on a soft 17, so that is not even a realistic option. It comes down to either doubling or drawing. While drawing is profitable and gives us the expectation to make money, doubling is even more profitable. And to win money in blackjack, we must take advantage of every profitable situation that presents itself to us.

With the 3, the dealer busts just enough and we make enough good hands with those small cards to make 17 vs. 3 a profitable double down in all blackjack games.

Did You Get it Right?   Yes! ☐   No ☐

SITUATION #34

We're playing <u>multiple</u> deck 21. The dealer has a 2 and we hold a soft 17. Stand, double, or draw?

Example Hand

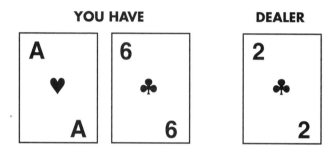

YOU HAVE   **DEALER**

THE RIGHT PLAY TO MAKE

Draw. In a multiple deck game, do not double down with A6 against the dangerous dealer upcard of 2. We don't have quite enough cannons with that soft 17 to go after the 2 aggressively as we would with the other dealer bust cards of 3-6. But at the same time, we are not going to stand with that lousy 17. So we'll draw. What's the worst that can happen: we draw badly and sit with a weak 16 as opposed to a slightly better but still weak 17? Not much to worry about.

In a single deck game though, with the removal of those three known cards, it is correct to double soft 17 vs. 2.

Did You Get it Right?   Yes! ☐   No ☐

SITUATION #35

We're playing <u>single</u> deck 21. The dealer has a 9 and we hold a soft 17. Stand or draw?

Example Hand

YOU HAVE		DEALER

THE RIGHT PLAY TO MAKE

Draw, draw, draw, draw, draw. We talked about it earlier but I see this bad play so often, it is worth showing the play yet one more time. With a 17 we are not going anywhere in life, particularly against dealer upcards that will make hands about 75% of the time.

If the 17 is hard, we can only hope the water recedes before the river overflows into the house. Nothing we can do. But if our 17 is soft, as it is here, we pile up the sandbags and see what we can do. We have to give ourselves a fighting chance.

Did You Get it Right?   Yes! ☐   No ☐

SITUATION #36

You have a potential doubling situation, A4, a soft 15 against a 5. Do you go for it or simply draw?

Example Hand

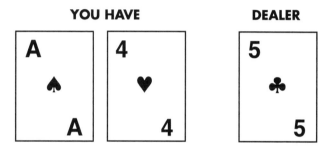

YOU HAVE   **DEALER**

THE RIGHT PLAY TO MAKE

Go for it. Double down. This is obviously more a play that takes advantage of the weakest dealer upcards with high busting potential than pushing our own strength (since the drawing of a ten value card to our hand does not improve it). There are four cards however, that will improve the totals to 18 or better, and one card that will make a 17, which is not much, but will help push a few hands.

We have a profitable double and don't want to miss the opportunity to double our bet. Double down with A4 and A5 against the weak upcards of, 4, 5, and 6.

Did You Get it Right?   Yes! ☐   No ☐

SITUATION #37

Here's another potential doubling situation: A5, a soft 16 against a 3. Double or draw?

Example Hand

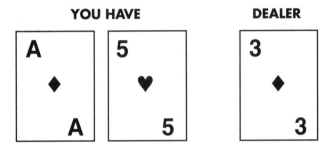

YOU HAVE

| A ♦ A | 5 ♥ 5 |

DEALER

| 3 ♦ 3 |

THE RIGHT PLAY TO MAKE

Draw. The 3, and even more so the 2, make too many hands to make this a profitable double down. Soft 15s (A4) and soft 16s (A5) can take advantage of the high busting potential of the 4, 5, and 6, but against the 2,3, drawing is the order of the day.

And if the situation doesn't call for a double, you sure don't want to be sitting there with a lousy 15 or 16 when you can improve at no risk of busting. These are clear situations of drawing.

Did You Get it Right?   Yes! ☐   No ☐

SITUATION #38

The dealer shows a mighty 10, we hold A4, a soft 15. What's the best play?

Example Hand

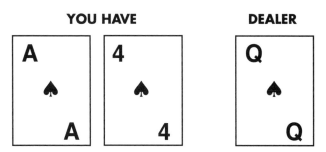

YOU HAVE   **DEALER**

A ♠ A   4 ♠ 4   Q ♠ Q

THE RIGHT PLAY TO MAKE

Hopefully, the correct play is second nature to you by now. If not, you need to study up some more. Drawing is the only play to consider. It does no good to stand, in fact it's terrible to do so when you have the possibility to improve with no risk of busting. And it would be even dumber to double down.

Did You Get it Right?   Yes! ☐   No ☐

SITUATION #39

Dealer has a 5, we hold a soft 13 (A2) or a soft 14 (A3). Double or draw?

Example Hand

YOU HAVE   **DEALER**

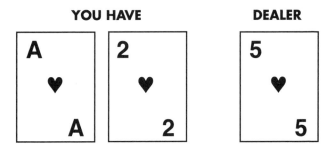

THE RIGHT PLAY TO MAKE

Double down with A2 and A3 against the dealer upcard of 5 as well as the 6. The A2 and A3 gives us a slightly favorable double down situation only against the two dealer upcards that bust the most, but no other upcards in a multiple deck game. (Note that in a single deck game you can also add the 4 as a correct double down.)

You have an advantage in these situations and want to squeeze a little more money from the table.

Did You Get it Right?   Yes! ☐   No ☐

SITUATION #40

We have a soft 13 (A2) or soft 14 (A3), the dealer has a 3. Double or draw?

Example Hand

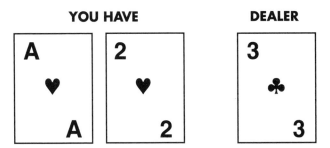

YOU HAVE		DEALER

THE RIGHT PLAY TO MAKE

Draw. This is not a doubling situation. The dealer makes too many hands with the 3 (and the 2) for doubling to be profitable.

Do not make the same mistake made by the really bad players who sometimes stand here. Never stand with these low soft totals. If you're not doubling down with these hands, you best be drawing.

Did You Get it Right?   Yes! ☐   No ☐

SITUATION #41

We have a soft 14 (A3), the dealer has a 9. Obviously doubling is bad, but is standing the correct play?

Example Hand

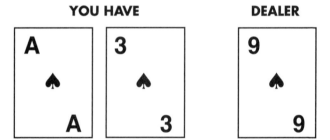

YOU HAVE		DEALER

THE RIGHT PLAY TO MAKE

No. Standing with soft 13 is not correct here or in any other situation. In fact, standing with a soft 13 against any dealer upcard is about as dumb a play as can be made. Doubling, as posed in the questions, is bad (though awful, stupid, or brain-dead) might be more apt.

The correct play is to draw.

Did You Get it Right?   Yes! ☐   No ☐

9

PLAY BY PLAY
SPLITTING

SITUATIONS 42-68

Splitting does two things for us: It allows us to take a profitable situation and double our bet with two hands, and it allows us to take one bad hand and split it into two improved hands with better chances on each.

There are many plays to keep track of here, making splitting the most difficult of all the Basic Strategies to remember. The key to remembering the correct plays though, is to understand the concepts behind them, and thus, to develop a blackjack "common sense."

I hope you're ready. There are many tricky and difficult plays ahead, in fact, 27 of them, so buckle up, and let's see what you got.

(Three quick tips: Always split 8s, never split 5s and 10s.)

SITUATION #42

We have a pair of sevens (77), the dealer has a 9. Split or draw? Or do we stand?

Example Hand

YOU HAVE   **DEALER**

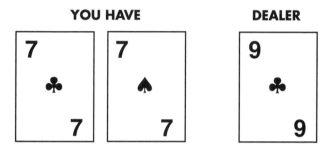

THE RIGHT PLAY TO MAKE

This is a draw situation. While you have a weak 14 against a strong 9, you certainly don't want to split this into two hands starting at 7 each and be faced with a second underdog situation. Similarly, you wouldn't split 7's against the 8, 10, or Ace either. Hoping for two potential 17s is not a pretty sight with double the money on the table against stronger dealer upcards.

Is standing an option here? Only as much as simply handing the dealer your money and saying "keep it." No, standing is not an intelligent option.

Did You Get it Right?   Yes! ☐   No ☐

SITUATION #43

Three 7s on the board, we have two of them, the dealer has the other. Stand, or draw? Or split?

Example Hand

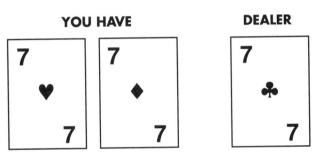

YOU HAVE		DEALER

THE RIGHT PLAY TO MAKE

Yes indeed. Split! Here's the deal. Our 14 stinks, and while two starting totals of 7 each isn't much, against a dealer's 7 we transform one loser into two potential pushes. Yup, splitting is the correct play.

Standing on 14 against a 7 is out and out dumb, and while drawing is better than standing, it is an awful play here when you have the option of splitting the 7s.

Did You Get it Right?   Yes! ☐   No ☐

SITUATION #44

We have 77 vs. 3. The 3 is a tricky card, the 7s are weak. Split, stand or draw?

Example Hand

YOU HAVE **DEALER**

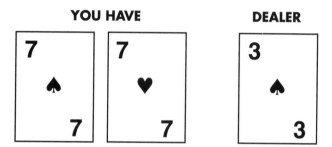

THE RIGHT PLAY TO MAKE

Splitting is correct. The basic element driving this play is the chance to break up a dead hand of 14 into two hands with improved possibilities, albeit not strong ones since we're only starting with 7s.

There is gain in splitting over standing. Split 77 vs. 3.

Did You Get it Right?   Yes! ☐   No ☐

SITUATION #45

We have 77 vs. 6. It looks like we can take advantage of that weak 6. Should we split?

Example Hand

YOU HAVE   **DEALER**

THE RIGHT PLAY TO MAKE

Split! If splitting 77 vs. 3 is a good play, 77 vs. 6 (and 77 vs. 4 or 5) is that much better. The dealer will be busting more than 40% of the time with 4, 5 or 6 as an upcard and we want to be in on the action, especially when we can break up that horrible 14.

This is a big gain play and should always be made.

Did You Get it Right?   Yes! ☐   No ☐

SITUATION #46

The dealer holds the dangerous 2 and we start with 77? Should we split?

Example Hand

YOU HAVE **DEALER**

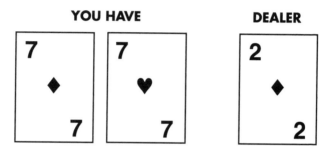

THE RIGHT PLAY TO MAKE

Yes, take advantage and split. As we know, a starting hand of 7 points by itself is not all that strong, but two hands of 7 each are a tremendous improvement over one hand of 14. Is starting with a 7 against a dealer's 2 much to get excited about? No, but it's much, much better than staying passive with the 14.

Splitting is correct here and against all dealer bust cards with a 77 hand.

Did You Get it Right? Yes! ☐ No ☐

SITUATION #47

The dealer's upcard is a 6. We have 88. This looks like a clear split. Am I right?

Example Hand

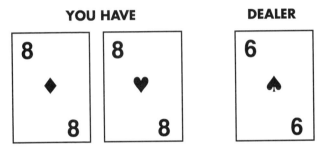

| YOU HAVE | | DEALER |

THE RIGHT PLAY TO MAKE

Yes you are. This is a clear split. You're taking the worst hard total possible, a 16, and making two starting totals of 8 each against the very weak dealer upcard of 6. It's a no-brainer.

Splitting 88 against all the bust cards, 2-6, is always a big gain. But what if the upcard is a 7? Aha, let's try that situation.

Did You Get it Right?   Yes! ☐   No ☐

SITUATION #48

The dealer's upcard is now a 7.
We have 88.
Split, stand, or draw?

Example Hand

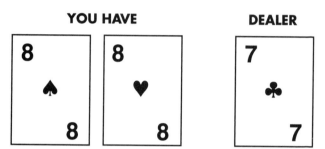

| YOU HAVE | | DEALER |

THE RIGHT PLAY TO MAKE

Split! Absolutely split, this is a huge gain play. You take the worst possible hand, a 16, and split it into two hands of 8 each that both have a winning expectation against the dealer's upcard of 7.

Standing against the 7 would be a terrible play; not splitting would be way worse. Split 88 vs. 7 *every* time you see it.

Did You Get it Right?　　Yes! ☐　　　　No ☐

SITUATION #49

We're dealt another 88, but this time the dealer has a 10. This is not a split but a clear draw. Correct?

Example Hand

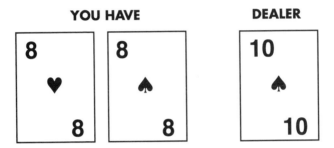

YOU HAVE		DEALER

THE RIGHT PLAY TO MAKE

Incorrect. Split 88 vs the 10 and the 9 and Ace as well. This is the strangest of all the Basic Strategy plays. Splitting 88 vs. 9, 10, and Ace, goes against the general concept of not making one bad hand into two, which this does. However, it is the better play than drawing (and certainly better than standing, of course).

Though splitting makes two very weak hands of 8 each against the powerful dealer upcards of 9, 10 and Ace, you improve upon the 16, our worst starting total. While we will lose very badly by splitting 88 here, we lose less badly than by not splitting. Do the lesser evil, split.

Did You Get it Right?   Yes! ☐   No ☐

SITUATION #50

One more 88 situation to consider. 88 vs. the dealer's 8. Hit, stand, or split?

Example Hand

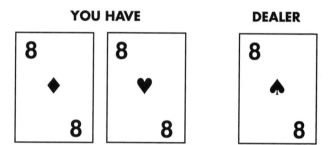

YOU HAVE   **DEALER**

THE RIGHT PLAY TO MAKE

Split again. We take the worst hand, 16, which has heavy loss expectations against the dealer's upcard of 8, in fact against any dealer's upcard, even the dealer bust cards of 2-6, and transform it into two starting hands of 8 each, both of which can push a dealer's possible 18. Those prospects are much brighter.

Split 88 against the dealer's 8 knowing that you have a huge gain.

Did You Get it Right?   Yes! ☐   No ☐

SITUATION #51

The big 10s. I see players split 10s all the time against the dealer's 6. Is it correct to split or stand?

Example Hand

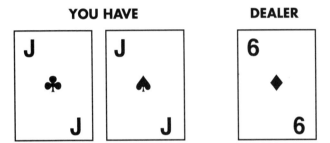

YOU HAVE		DEALER
J ♣ J	J ♠ J	6 ♦ 6

THE RIGHT PLAY TO MAKE

Stand! Forget about the randoms out there who make this play and countless other bonehead moves. You virtually have the casino's money in the bank with a very powerful 20–leave it there.

This is not a split situation, nor is 10-10 against any dealer upcard, not for players who want to beat the casino and win money.

Did You Get it Right? Yes! ☐   No ☐

SITUATION #52

You have Aces, a great hand. Dealer also has an Ace. I heard I should always split. True?

Example Hand

YOU HAVE
DEALER

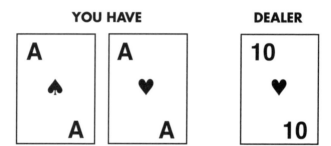

THE RIGHT PLAY TO MAKE

Very true. Always split Aces. What's not to like about two starting hands of 11 points each? It doesn't matter what the dealer shows as an upcard, splitting AA is always correct. You would have to be unfamiliar with the game or brain-dead to draw and not split with AA.

Note two things about split Aces: First, most casinos don't allow resplitting of Aces (the resplit into a third Ace hand should a third Ace be drawn–though you can still draw more cards to the AA) and second, the draw of a 10 to the split Ace is a 21 only, not a blackjack.

Did You Get it Right?   Yes! ☐   No ☐

SITUATION #53

You have 99, the dealer has a powerful 10 for an upcard. Is this a split? A stand?

Example Hand

YOU HAVE   **DEALER**

THE RIGHT PLAY TO MAKE

Stand. While 18 is not the strongest hand, particularly against a 10, it can only lose once. You don't want two 9s against a potential 20 and you certainly don't want to draw with a hard 18! (Soft 18, A7, is another story though.)

Stand with 99 vs. the dealer's 10 and also against the dealer's Ace. They're too powerful to break up the 9s into separate hands.

Did You Get it Right?   Yes! ☐   No ☐

SITUATION #54

You have 99, the dealer has the weak 5 for an upcard. Do you take the automatic win by standing?

Example Hand

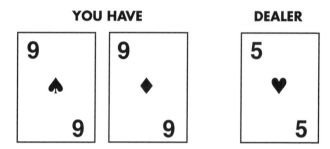

YOU HAVE

DEALER

THE RIGHT PLAY TO MAKE

No way Jose, not with this great hand. This is a big time split play. Yeah, the 18 is nice against the 5, but two hands of 9 each is powerful and more important, very profitable. Don't ever hesitate to make this split, it is integral to the winning straegy.

Split 99 against all the dealer's big bust cards, the 4, 5 and 6. How about the 2 and 3 though? Let's see...

Did You Get it Right?   Yes! ☐   No ☐

SITUATION #55

With the same 99 for the player, the dealer holds the dangerous 2. Split or stand?

Example Hand

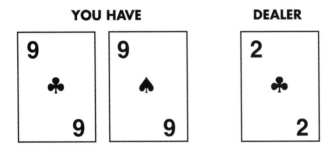

YOU HAVE   **DEALER**

THE RIGHT PLAY TO MAKE

Split again. While the 2 is one of the dealer's bust cards, it is dangerous because it will not only bust less often than the 3, 4, 5 and 6, but it will make an 18 or better more than half the time. However, two starting totals of 9 each puts us in a potentially stronger position with double the money out on the table, which we like, for the advantage is with us. This is a profitable split and should always be made.

Double 99 against 2 and the dealer 3. In fact, double down with 99 against all the dealer bust cards, the 2, 3, 4, 5 and 6.

Did You Get it Right?   Yes! ☐   No ☐

SITUATION #56

We're dealt a 99, the dealer has an upcard of 8. The correct play: Split or stand?

Example Hand

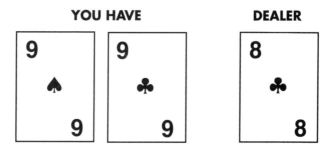

YOU HAVE   **DEALER**

THE RIGHT PLAY TO MAKE

Split! Our 18 against a potential 18 is a push, not bad, but definitely inferior to two starting totals of 9 each, both potential winners. This is a profitable situation, which is why we want more money on the table in the form of the second split hand.

The correct and profitable basic strategy play is to split 99 against the dealer's 8.

Did You Get it Right?   Yes! ☐   No ☐

SITUATION #57

Here is an interesting play. We have 99, the dealer has a 7. Split or stand?

Example Hand

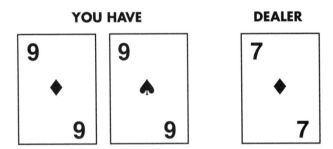

YOU HAVE		DEALER
9 ♦ 9	9 ♠ 9	7 ♦ 7

THE RIGHT PLAY TO MAKE

Stand! "What?" you may ask. "I should should double down against the 8 but not the 7, a weaker upcard?" Yes, that's right. Here's the reason. If the dealer turns over a 10 for a hole card, we're a winner, 18 against 17. This would be every bit as powerful as holding a 20 against a dealer's 19. Given this powerful edge, we'll take a bird in the hand for the two in the bush.

In blackjack, we always play the overwhelming favorite, unless of course, we have a hand with more overwhelming profitable possibilities. That's not the case here.

Did You Get it Right?   Yes! ☐   No ☐

SITUATION #58

Here is another interesting play. We have 99, the dealer has a 9. Split or stand?

Example Hand

YOU HAVE **DEALER**

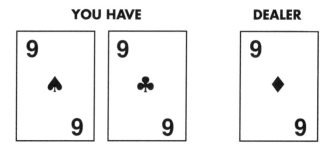

THE RIGHT PLAY TO MAKE

Split. Sitting with an 18 against a potential dealer's 19 is not the best news. However, breaking the hand into two hands starting totals of 9 points each puts us on a much better footing—indeed!

These 99 splits are logical plays that make sense if you really think about them. They are computer tested and mathematically correct, so have no hesitation to make the split plays as listed in the Basic Strategy.

Did You Get it Right?   Yes! ☐   No ☐

SITUATION #59

We hold 22, and the dealer shows an 8 for an upcard
Split or draw? Or stand?

Example Hand

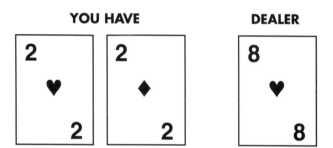

YOU HAVE   **DEALER**

THE RIGHT PLAY TO MAKE

This is a draw. Standing on only four points? That's about as dumb a play as you can make, and I've seen it. This is not a split though. We don't want two hands starting out with only 2 points with the dealer's possible 18 towering over us. Better to start with one inferior hand of four points, than two hands of two points each.

Draw 22 against the dealer's 8, 9, 10 and Ace. These dealer totals are too powerful to voluntarily risk an additional bet with starting totals of 2 points. We'll play the four, thank you very much.

Did You Get it Right?   Yes! ☐   No ☐

SITUATION #60

We hold a hand of 22, and the dealer shows a 7 for an upcard. Split or draw?

Example Hand

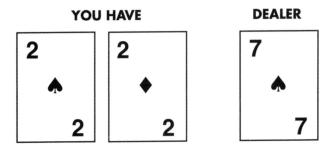

YOU HAVE		DEALER

THE RIGHT PLAY TO MAKE

Guess what? This is a split. While the dealer's 7 will end up making a lot of hands, it will tend to make weaker totals than the other pat cards, in particular, 17s, which is a really weak total. Splitting 22 against the dealer's 7 is a very large gain for us, especially considering that we'll make an 18 or better more than half the time starting with a 2.

Don't be scared by the 7. It's a weak card and we have the edge here. In addition to the 22, we'll also double down with 33 vs. the dealer's 7.

Did You Get it Right?   Yes! ☐   No ☐

SITUATION #61

We hold a hand of 33, the dealer shows a 4 for an upcard Split or draw?

Example Hand

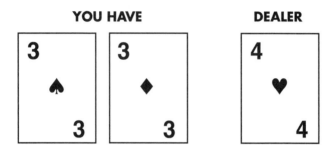

YOU HAVE		DEALER
3 ♠ 3	3 ♦ 3	4 ♥ 4

THE RIGHT PLAY TO MAKE

Split. While a starting total of three points each in a hand is not much to write home about, it's a lot better than starting with six points, or for that matter, four or five points. But the real reason for this split is that the dealer is gong to bust often with that 4. That combined with the good hands we will sometimes achieve, makes this play a big gain over simply drawing.

Similarly, split 33 against the weakest dealer upcards of 5 and 6 as well as the 7. That goes for the player's 22 also. To sum up, split 22 and 33 against dealer upcards of 4, 5, 6 and 7.

Did You Get it Right?   Yes! ☐   No ☐

SITUATION #62

Three deuces aboard. We hold 22, and the dealer shows a third 2. Split or draw?

Example Hand

YOU HAVE   **DEALER**

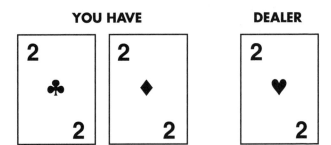

THE RIGHT PLAY TO MAKE

Draw. The dealer's 2 is too dangerous to double our table wager through splitting. 22 versus the dealer's 2 is a whole different situation than 22 versus other dealer bust cards. Each point higher than the 2 is one more card that will bust the dealer should a 10 be in the hole. For example, if the dealer holds a 12, only 10s will bust him. But if he holds a 13, now there are the 9s that can bust him as well, while 8s will also bust a hard 14. The more likely a dealer is to bust, the more aggressive we puruse our doubling and splitting plays.

Draw 22 and 33 vs. the dealer's 2. Do not split.

Did You Get it Right?   Yes! ☐   No ☐

SITUATION #63

In a **multiple** deck game, we have a pair of deuces, 22, and the dealer has a 3. What's the play?

Example Hand

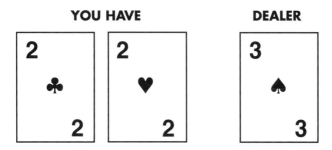

YOU HAVE	DEALER

THE RIGHT PLAY TO MAKE

Draw. The dealer's three like the dealer's 2 doesn't quite bust enough to make this a profitable split. Thus, with 22 and 33 as well, draw don't split against the dealer's 2 and 3 as upcards. To sum up, split 22 and 33 against dealer upcards of 4-7, simply draw against all other upcards.

Note that in a single deck game, it is correct to split 22 against the dealer's 3, but in all other situations, the correct splitting strategy is as stated above.

Did You Get it Right?   Yes! ☐   No ☐

SITUATION #64

It's a <u>multiple</u> deck game, we have 44, the dealer has a 5. What's the best play–split, hit, or even double?

Example Hand

YOU HAVE   **DEALER**

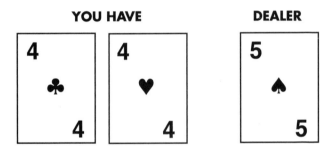

THE RIGHT PLAY TO MAKE

Draw. One of the cardinal splitting rules states that you don't split fours.* Eight points is not a powerful start, but it is at least decent. Four points, on the other hand, stinks. At twice the bet, it is even a worse concept. Doubling 8 vs. 5 is not a good play in multiple deck games, so again, drawing is the best play here.**

Draw 44 against all dealer upcards.

* When doubling after splitting is allowed, 4s will be split against the dealer's 5 and 6 only.
**In single deck, double down 44 against 5 and 6.

Did You Get it Right?   Yes! ☐   No ☐

SITUATION #65

We're dealt a pair of 5s. The dealer holds a weak 6. Should we split or simply hit?

Example Hand

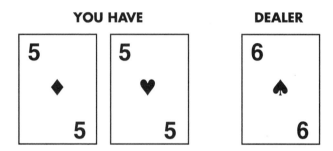

YOU HAVE   **DEALER**

THE RIGHT PLAY TO MAKE

Neither! Doubling down is the correct play. Five plus five is ten points, a great starting total. Only a fool would make two horrible hands of five each out of this powerful start. Drawing is a possibility but with so much less profitability than doubling down, it would be a foolish play when you can get double your money out on the felt with such a great advantage. You got the goods, strut 'em.

55 is a clear double down against dealer upcards of 2-9, and a simple draw against the 10 and Ace. But never split this hand.

Did You Get it Right?   Yes! ☐   No ☐

SITUATION #66

We have two sixes, the dealer holds
an upcard of seven points.
Split, stand, or draw?

Example Hand

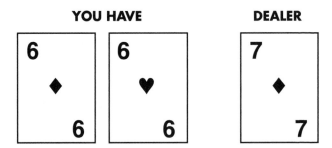

YOU HAVE   **DEALER**

THE RIGHT PLAY TO MAKE

Drawing is correct here. First, you don't want to split and make two awful starting hands of 6 each–the worst starting cards–against an upcard that will give the dealer hands 75% of the time. That would be suicide. Second, you have to be a really bad player to stand on 12 vs. any dealer upcard of 7 or higher. That's just a terrible percentage play.

That leaves drawing as the best and most sensible option, not only with 66 versus the dealer's 7, but against all the dealer pat cards, the 7, 8, 9, 10 and Ace.

Did You Get it Right?   Yes! ☐   No ☐

SITUATION #67

We have two sixes, the dealer holds a 4 as an upcard. Split, draw, or stand?

Example Hand

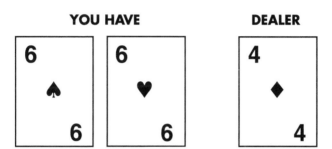

YOU HAVE		DEALER

THE RIGHT PLAY TO MAKE

Split. This is a horse of a different color than when the dealer has a 7 as an upcard. Starting with two hands of 6 is of no great shakes but it is a gain over the one hand of 12 due to the high busting potential of the 4. This is yet another example of making more aggressive plays against the weakest dealer upcards. Drawing is obviousy not a good option as we wouldn't want to bust against a dealer's 4. That's simply bad strategy.

It is correct to split 44, 55, and 66 against the dealer's 3, 4, 5 and 6. And how about the dangerous 2?

Did You Get it Right?   Yes! ☐   No ☐

SITUATION #68

Multiple deck. We have 66, but now the dealer holds the dangerous 2. Split or draw? Or stand?

Example Hand

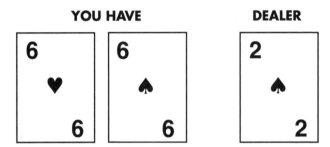

YOU HAVE		DEALER
6 ♥ 6	6 ♠ 6	2 ♠ 2

THE RIGHT PLAY TO MAKE

Draw, do not split, do not stand. The dealer makes just too many hands starting with that dangerous deuce and thus we must respect its power and opt out of the split. There is loss, not gain by splitting.* Should we stand then? Normally, we don't want to bust when the dealer has a chance of busting, but the combination of our 12 busting less (less risky to draw) and the dealer busting less with his own 2, makes drawing 12 vs. 2 (and 3) a drawing situation, not a standing one. So, in multiple deck 21, hit 66 vs. 2, but split 66 vs. 3-6.

*Note: In single deck, it is correct to split 66 vs. 2 as well.

Did You Get it Right?   Yes! ☐   No ☐

10

PLAY BY PLAY
INSURANCE

SITUATIONS 69-70

Insurance is a bet offered by the casino that players either look at as a way to protect their good hands or to go with their hunches and walk away from bad hands without losing their bets.

Blackjack is rife with fallacies, and to make money, you must dispel with any incorrect notions you have about strategy, and learn to make the best percentage plays. That's the only way you're going to be a winner at the game. We have two situations in this section to test you on, and to expose commonly-believed insurance fallacies for what they really are.

After these two situations, it will be time to add up your scores from the five play-by-play chapters and see how you hold up against our challenge.

Okay then, take two...

SITUATION #69

The dealer shows an Ace and asks if we want insurance. Take insurance or decline?

Example Hand

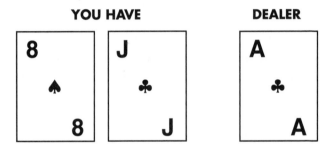

YOU HAVE		DEALER

THE RIGHT PLAY TO MAKE

Do not take insurance, it is a bad bet. Unless you're a card counter and know that the situation is ten-rich, it is never correct to take insurance. There are 36 non-tens and 16 tens in a full deck, four each of the 10s, Js, Qs, and Ks. If you take insurance, that is a 36-16 ratio, yet you are only getting paid 2-1 (32-16). By removing the above three cards, the ratio gets worse, down to 34 non-tens, which would lose your insurance bet if drawn, and only 15 tens, which would win. We're still only paid 2-1 (30-15) to draw a ten, but the proper odds on this bet is 34-15. That advantage goes to the casino. To win you have to play tough blackjack. No insurance!

Did You Get it Right?　　Yes! ☐　　　　No ☐

SITUATION #70

Blackjack! However, the dealer also shows an Ace. We're advised to "insure" the blackjack. Good advice?

Example Hand

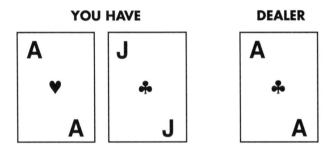

YOU HAVE		DEALER
A ♥ A	J ♣ J	A ♣ A

THE RIGHT PLAY TO MAKE

No. The advice is well intentioned, but it is not correct for the same reasons we just discussed. Unless you're a card counter and know that the situation is ten-rich, it is never correct to insure a blackjack. Forget about "insuring" your blackjack. The real concept to understand is that insurance is a *separate* bet and it is a bad one. If you want to beat the casino at blackjack you have to play smart on every single play. The times you deviate from correct play, are the times you give the edge back to the house and join the multitudes of losers at a game that can be beat. Again, unless you know the deck is ten rich, do not take insurance.

Did You Get it Right?   Yes! ☐   No ☐

11

FIVE BONEHEAD PLAYS

PLAYS 1-5

In this chapter, are five bonehead moves I have seen players make at the blackjack tables. You see these moves sometimes and wonder: what were these players thinking?

Not only are these dumb moves that rank among the worst plays you can find in blackjack, the odds they buck compete with the worse percentages you can find in any casino game.

I have chosen these five bonehead plays somewhat for their instructive value and somewhat for their entertainment value. At the same time, I managed to squeeze in a few more lessons on money management, a message I hope you have received from me loud and clear by now.

There is enough material on this dubious topic that I could easily have made this chapter '10 Bonehead Moves' or even devoted an entire book to this subject, but in any case, let's now take a look and see what our gallery has to offer us.

BONEHEAD MOVE #1

A young guy, obviously drunk, got dealt a 12 with a large bet on the felt. He decided to double down!

The Hand

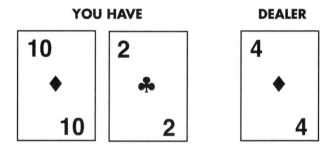

YOU HAVE		DEALER
10 ◆ 10	2 ♣ 2	4 ◆ 4

THE RIGHT PLAY TO MAKE

The correct play of course, is to stand, but this luminary found a creative way to play this hand. The dealer had to ask the player *twice* if this was what he really wanted to do. "Yes, I want to double," said this burly man in his thirties. "I have a feeling." I had a feeling too and sure enough, the player drew a 10, busted out at double the money, and then watched as the dealer turned over a nine for a 13, then drew another nine and busted.

He cursed the dealer, bet the rest of a large pile in front of him, and quickly lost that as the dealer drew a blackjack. At no point in time or dreams does any hard hand of 12 points or higher make sense to double. Any 10 value card will bust the hand at double the loss.

BONEHEAD MOVE #2

An elderly lady, in the midst of losing about $300 she looked like she needed, had the hand below.

The Hand

YOU HAVE		DEALER

THE RIGHT PLAY TO MAKE

She drew and to no one's surprise, she busted. Obviously, the correct play is to stand. There are only three reasons to draw in this situation:

1. You know that the next card is an A, 2, 3 or 4.

2. You know the dealer has a higher total than you which means you will surely lose.

3. There is something wrong with your mental state of mind—temporarily or permanently.

I suppose there are other reasons to draw: the player could be from another planet, or a deceased relative could have passed the holy word that this somehow must be done, but in any case, hitting on a hard 17 or higher is suicide and a pure bonehead move.

BONEHEAD MOVE #3

I watched one day, as an old-timer managed to get wiped out in just a few hours. Was it any wonder?

The Hand

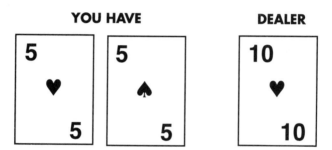

YOU HAVE		DEALER
5 ♥ 5	5 ♠ 5	10 ♥ 10

THE RIGHT PLAY TO MAKE

This guy thought he knew it all, but what he knew in life, certainly had nothing to do with whatever was happening at the table. Think of some bad moves. Standing? That's a dumb play. Doubling down? That's even worse. But he found an even dumber possibility. He split! Of course, the correct move is to simply draw.

A starting hand of 10 is a strong starting point as the draw of a 10 makes a 20, a powerful hand. But breaking this up into two miserable starting totals of 5 each is a true bonehead move and then compounding this idiocy by splitting them against a 10, of all cards, really earns a proud march in the parade of bonehead moves.

BONEHEAD MOVE #4

A young man was seemingly winning every hand until this fateful move turned the tide.

The Hand

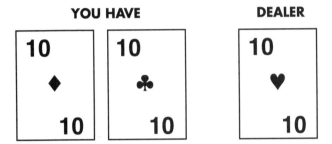

YOU HAVE		DEALER
10 ♦ 10	10 ♣ 10	10 ♥ 10

THE RIGHT PLAY TO MAKE

Most players would automatically stand. There is nothing to think about. But this young man, whose ego was frothing over like steamed milk in an overfilled cup, was high on a winning roll and thought he could do no wrong, that is, until he split the 10s to the accompaniment of groans from fellow players, and then lost both hands to a 19. That was the beginning of a hard slide that took every penny of his winnings from the table. He then dug into his wallet for more, twice, losing all that too, violating another cardinal rule in blackjack. This horrible ten split is made too often by players who just don't know better. If you were dealt a 20 every hand for 24 hours, you could retire–permanently.

BONEHEAD MOVE #5

Sadly, this bonehead move happens all too often, but what can you say about people like this anyway?

The Hand

YOU HAVE   **DEALER**

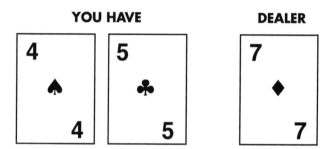

THE RIGHT PLAY TO MAKE

Rather than drawing, the correct play, this player doubled down, drew a 10, a great draw, but watched the dealer turn over a 3, then a 4, and another 6 to beat him. While in itself this play is bad, it was the circumstances surrounding this play that was the real bonehead move. I had been watching this player for several hours. He was drunk and rude to the dealers every time he lost a hand, which was frequently, but they put up with him because of the large amount of money he was betting. I watched him drop over $20,000 during that time, and at the end, a pitboss, despite the abuse he had received, gave the poor sap a few dollars out of his pocket so he could take a bus home and watch his kids. Need I say more?

12

ANOTHER WORD ON MONEY MANAGEMENT

Losing money on a dumb play is one thing, and we saw a few examples of that in the Bonehead Moves chapter, but losing money you *need* for real living situations is a matter on an entirely different level.

Too many people gamble with money that should be directed at basic needs and end up destroying their lives. The answers they need are not in any of the strategy sections in this book but with professional help. If you find yourself losing money you cannot afford to lose, stay away from gambling, far away, and if necessary, get help as well. Don't destroy your life for some quick, ephemeral, and dubious pleasure.

If this rings a bell, even on a smaller scale, your problem may be deeper than you can deal with solo. It is one thing to destroy your own life, it is another to destroy the lives of people and family around you who depend on the money you lose gambling. If you've got issues, deal with them, and not only stop gambling but physically stay away from its temptations. Life is full of good possibilities, see what you can find out there.

Play smart and be smart; that is what this book is about.

13

THE SCORECARD

Here's a place where you can tally up the scores from the 70 situations presented in chapters 6 through 10 and see how you did. Add 'em up.

CHAPTER	RIGHT	WRONG
HITTING AND STANDING	_____	_____
HARD DOUBLING	_____	_____
SOFT DOUBLING	_____	_____
SPLITTING	_____	_____
INSURANCE	_____	_____
TOTAL	_____	_____

I have provided another tally sheet on the reverse side of this page so you can go through another time and improve your score if you weren't perfect the first time.

The scorecard on the following page gives the grades. I expect you to reach perfection. You'll see there is not room for many errors to get my high grade. I take winning seriously, you should too! Let's see how you did.

THE SCORECARD

RIGHT
70	Perfect, you can hang with Cardoza.
68-69	Excellent, you're almost a top notch player.
66-67	Very good. But keep working at it.
65-66	Borderline. These plays are starting to cost you money.
60-64	Not good. You're not ready for the tables. Learn more.
55-59	The casinos are in love with you.
54/less	Don't go anywhere near a game until you get up to par.

If your first time through the situations didn't get you into the top levels, let's try again and measure your improvement. Our goal: A perfect 70.

SECOND TIME THROUGH

CHAPTER	RIGHT	WRONG
HITTING AND STANDING	_____	_____
HARD DOUBLING	_____	_____
SOFT DOUBLING	_____	_____
SPLITTING	_____	_____
INSURANCE	_____	_____
TOTAL	_____	_____

14

THE GLOSSARY

Barring a Player - The exclusion of a player from the blackjack tables.

Basic Strategy - The optimal playing strategy for a particular set of rules and number of decks used, assuming the player has knowledge of only his own two cards and the dealer's upcard.

Blackjack or Natural - An original two card holding consisting of an Ace and ten-value card. Also the name of the game.

Break - see Bust.

Burn Card - A card, usually from the top of the deck, that is removed from play. The top card is traditionally *burned* after a fresh shuffle and before the cards are dealt.

Bust or Break - To exceed the total of 21, a loser.

Card Counting - A method of keeping track of the cards already played so that knowledge of the remaining cards can be used to adjust strategies. A player that counts cards is called a *card counter*.

Composition of the Deck - A term used to describe the particular makeup of the cards remaining in the deck.

Composition Change - As cards are removed from the deck, the normal proportion of certain cards to other groups of cards change. This is called a composition change.

Dealer - The casino employee who deals the cards, makes the proper payoffs to winning hands and collects lost bets.

Doubling, Doubling Down - A player option to double the original bet after seeing his original two cards. If the player chooses this option, one additional card will be dealt.

Doubling after Splitting - A favorable player option offered in only some US and international casinos whereby players are allowed to double down after splitting a pair (according to normal doubling rules).

Draw - see Hit.

Early Surrender - An option to forfeit a hand and lose half the bet before the dealer checks for a blackjack.

Exposed Card - see Upcard.

Eye in the Sky - Refers to the mirrors above the gaming tables where the games are constantly supervised to protect both the player and the house from being cheated.

Face Card - Also known as **Paint**. A Jack, Queen or King.

First Base - Seat closest to the dealer's left. The first baseman acts upon his hand first.

Flat Bet - To bet the same amount every hand.

Hard Total - A hand without an Ace or if containing an Ace, where the Ace counts as only 1 point (10, 6, A).

Hit - The act of drawing (requesting) a card from the dealer.

Hole Card - The dealer's unexposed downcard.

House - A term to denote the Casino.

Insurance - A side bet that can be made when the dealer shows an Ace. The player wagers up to half his original bet and gets paid 2 to 1 on that bet if the dealer shows a blackjack. If the dealer does not have a blackjack, the insurance bet is lost.

Multiple Deck Game - Blackjack played with two or more decks of cards, usually referring to a 4, 6 or 8 deck game.

Natural - see Blackjack.

Nickels - $5 chips, usually red in color.

Pat Card - A dealer upcard of 7 through Ace, that tends to give the dealer pat hands.

Pat Hand - A hand totaling 17-21.

Pit Boss - Casino employee who supervises play at the tables.

Push - A tie between the dealer and the player.

Quarters - $25 chips, usually green in color.

Shoe - An oblong box used to hold multiple decks of cards.

Shuffle, Shuffling Up - The mixing of cards by a dealer prior to a fresh round of play.

Silver - $1 tokens or dollar chips.

Single Deck Game - Blackjack played from a single pack of cards.

Soft Hands, Soft Total - Hand in which the Ace counts as 11 points.

Splitting Pairs - A player option to split two cards of identical value so that two separate hands are formed. A bet equal to the original wager is placed next to the second hand.

Stand, Stand Pat - A player's decision not to draw a card.

Stiff Card - A dealer upcard of 2 through 6, that leaves the dealer with a high busting potential.

Stiff Hand - A hand totaling hard 12, 13, 14, 15 or 16; can be busted if hit.

Surrender, Late Surrender - A player option to forfeit his original hand and lose half the bet after it has been determined that the dealer does not have a blackjack.

Ten Factor - Refers to the concentration of tens in the deck.

Ten-Value Card - 10, Jack, Queen or King.

Third Base - Also called **Anchorman.** Position closest to the dealer's right. The third baseman makes the last play before the dealer's turn.

Toke or Tip - A gratuity either given or bet for the dealer.

Unit - Bet size used as a standard of measurement.

Upcard - The dealer's face up (exposed) card.

142

143